The EASY-CARE GARDENING EXPERT

Dr. D.G. Hessayon

First edition: 200,000 copies
Published 1996
by Expert Books
a division of Transworld Publishers Ltd

A catalogue record for this book is available from the British Library

TRANSWORLD PUBLISHERS LTD
61–63 Uxbridge Road, London W5 5SA

Distributed in the United States
by Sterling Publishing Co. Inc.,
387 Park Avenue South,
New York, NY 10016–8810

Distributed in Canada by
Cavendish Books Inc.,
Unit 5, 801 West 1st Street,
North Vancouver, B.C. V7P 1A4

EXPERT BOOKS

Contents

Printed and bound in Great Britain by Jarrold & Sons Ltd, Norwich

ISBN 0 903505 44 4

© D.G.HESSAYON 1996

CHAPTER 1

INTRODUCTION

About half of the gardens in this country are looked after by people who either like or positively enjoy the work involved in caring for their plots. For these dedicated millions the long hours spent mowing, hoeing, pruning, bedding out, pulling weeds and the rest are not regarded as either time-wasting or exhausting activities. For the dedicated and active gardener the traditional jobs are pleasurable pursuits which ensure that their much-loved land is kept in order — the work provides healthy exercise for those in sedentary jobs and peace of mind for people whose lives are filled with stress. To guide and inspire them there are countless books, numerous videos, some magazines and several TV series, but this book is not designed for them.

This book is for that often-ignored group, the reluctant or restricted gardener. The fundamental fact is that half of all gardens belong to people who do not like gardening, or who do not have enough time for gardening, or who do not have the health or strength for active gardening.

These people who need an easy-care approach to gardening are an extremely varied group. There are the lazy ones, of course, who do not like any form of physical work, but they make up only a small section of the reluctant or restricted gardener population. Much more numerous are those who just do not have the time to look after the garden adequately — children, job pressure or other hobbies take priority. There are also the aged, the infirm, the injured and the sick who would like to do more work on their beds, borders and lawns but cannot do so.

The good news for the reluctant or restricted gardener is that the easy-care approach described on the following pages can provide a garden which is attractive and has a well-tended appearance. Neat, colourful and weed-free, yet it will require only 10 to 50 per cent of the effort and time needed to maintain a standard garden with its beds of annuals, herbaceous border, vegetable garden, disease-prone roses and scattered containers.

This may sound too good to be true but there are a couple of provisos, as there is no such thing as a no-work method of gardening. First, there may be things to do in order to change the design so that you can get rid of time-wasting features and time-wasting plants. Secondly, never confuse easy-care gardening with neglect. The tasks involved may be easier than those associated with traditional gardening, but they must be done properly at the right time and in the right way.

CHAPTER 2
BASIC PRINCIPLES

There is one key point which must be cleared up right at the start. Easy-care gardening does not mean spending less time and effort on all the jobs you are doing now. To cut the lawn every two weeks instead of weekly and to take less care when planting shrubs is not the answer — doing less of the same old jobs means that in quite a short time the garden will look neglected.

Easy-care means adopting a new way of gardening whereby the great time-wasters are reduced or eliminated. These time-wasters are digging, weeding, watering, pruning and lawn edging. There is no magic formula to do this — it is simply a matter of using the four cornerstones of easy-care gardening set out on page 5 to support your wish to have a good garden with less effort.

Each cornerstone is vital, and the easy-care approach has been helped by advances in plant breeding and horticultural chemistry. Selecting easy-care plants is one of the cornerstones, and nowadays it has been made easier by the introduction of more disease-resistant plants and dwarf versions of lanky old favourites. These plants have to be fed, and slow-release fertilizers which last all season long are a great help when time for gardening is short. Healthy plants which need little attention are part of the story, but you have to stop weeds growing between them, and that is the role of ground cover. Mulching is a technique you are going to have to learn if you want to cut down on both weeding and watering, and for the weeds which may get through there are some excellent selective weedkillers to help you.

Not many people can begin from scratch and so create a garden filled with easy-care features from the start. But there is a great deal you can do to improve things in an established garden — read the section on Creating an Easy-care Design on pages 12–15 and apply as many of the principles as you can. Note the value of 'hard' landscaping (the use of non-living surfaces) with evergreens to provide year-round colour with virtually no maintenance.

A final thought. An easy-care garden is a place with an overall beauty — it is not an exhibition of individual showy blooms which must be cut once their charm starts to fade. Be tolerant — do not worry about the occasional weed in the lawn or the couple of plants which are not flourishing. The easy-care garden with its ground cover, year-round colour, attractive paths and patios and reliance on woody plants is so often better to look at and not just easier to maintain than the traditional work-intensive one.

THE FOUR CORNERSTONES OF EASY-CARE GARDENING

GIVE THE PLANTS A SUITABLE HOME
pages 6–7

CHOOSE EASY-CARE PLANTS
pages 8–11

PUT GROUND COVER AROUND THE PLANTS
page 11

CREATE AN EASY-CARE DESIGN
pages 12–15

Key to symbols used in the chapters on easy-care plants & techniques

✔ A plant or technique which is suitable for the easy-care garden

✘ A plant or technique which is not suitable for the easy-care garden

? A plant or technique which can be used in the easy-care garden but some risk or extra work is involved

Gardening Which? Low-maintenance garden is one of a series of theme gardens at Capel Manor near Enfield in North London. The garden consists of a small lawn (including mowing strip) and patio with raised beds and pond, plus borders filled with sun-loving ground cover plants and mulched with a thick layer of chipped bark and large pebbles

GIVE THE PLANTS A SUITABLE HOME

You can pick from many thousands of garden plants and you can select from all sorts of garden designs, but you cannot choose your soil. In nearly all cases some improvement is required before putting in new plants. If the soil is really poor then leaving it alone will involve you with extra work and expense later on. The display will be disappointing, but in addition the lack of vigorous growth and spread will mean that a considerable amount of ground cover will be essential around the stems. Some plant failure will be inevitable, and so there will be the cost and effort of replacement. There are three points to think about to ensure that the plants will have a satisfactory home — soil improvement, proper site selection and feeding.

Soil Improvement

If you are lucky you will have a medium-textured or loamy soil. It will have a good crumb structure and all you will have to do is to put on some form of humus mulch (see page 98) around the plants to maintain the organic content and to reduce the need for weeding and watering. Most soils, however, are either clayey or sandy — see below.

<table>
<tr>
<td>Squeeze a handful of moist soil. It forms a strong ball — when pressed it changes shape but does not fall apart. This ball feels smooth and sticky when wet. Stains the skin</td>
<td>Squeeze a handful of moist soil. When released it sifts through the fingers. A small sample feels gritty when rubbed between finger and thumb. Does not stain the skin</td>
</tr>
<tr>
<td>

HEAVY (Clayey) SOIL
Good points: Generally well supplied with plant foods which are not leached away by rain. Good water retention.
Bad points: Difficult to cultivate under most conditions. Cakes and cracks in dry weather — may waterlog in wet weather. Cold — flowers and vegetables appear later than average.

•

If the plot has not been cultivated before then dig thoroughly in autumn (see page 88) to expose the clods to winter frost — a generous quantity of organic matter should be incorporated at this time. Apply lime if the soil is acid or gypsum if it is not to improve the structure. Do not plant out until the soil is reasonably dry. Mulch established plants.

</td>
<td>

LIGHT (Sandy) SOIL
Good points: Easy to work, even when wet. Free-draining in winter. Warm — suitable for early flowers and vegetables.
Bad points: Usually short of plant foods. Frequent watering is necessary in summer or shallow-rooted plants may die. Cools down rapidly at night.

•

Water and food shortage are regular problems during the growing season. The structure is generally poor — lack of organic matter means that the soil is not crumbly. Digging is not the answer — the solution is to incorporate plenty of humus-making material into the top few inches in late winter or early spring. Mulching is vital to conserve moisture and reduce leaching of plant nutrients.

</td>
</tr>
</table>

The basic way to improve soil structure is to add a **humus maker**. These are bulky organic materials which are attacked by bacteria — the tiny organisms produce heat and also true humus, a magical material which cements clay or sand particles together to form soil crumbs. Not all humus makers, however, are equally effective in producing true humus.

Raw humus makers are efficient. These organic materials contain sufficient nutrients to stimulate active bacterial growth in the soil. Examples include fresh grass clippings, fresh dung and dug-in weeds. Heat is produced and soil structure is improved, but roots can be damaged and a nitrogen fertilizer has to be added. **Matured humus makers** such as well-rotted compost or manure are better — the true humus has been formed by bacterial action before the material is put into the soil. **Fibrous materials** such as peat act as sponges and open up the soil, but they create very little bacterial activity and so are poor humus makers. A humus maker which contains some plant nutrients is called a manure.

Proper site selection

If you have a large garden with patches of both acid and non-acid soil and situations which are both sunny and shady, then you can afford to buy plants on impulse at the garden centre knowing that you will be able to find a suitable site. For gardeners without this luxury it is essential to check the site needs of the plant before you buy it.

- Does it need acid soil?
- Does it need a sunny spot?
- Does it need a sheltered location?
- Does it need light land?

- Will it grow too tall/wide when mature?
- Will it grow tall/wide enough when mature?
- Does it need better drainage than is available?
- Does it need moist or boggy soil?

It happens to all of us. We see a plant in a pot or catalogue which is just what we are looking for, but the description makes it clear that the site we have available is quite unsuitable. We can then make one or other mistake. The first is to assume that the planting advice is far too strict or wrong, so we go ahead anyway. The second one is that we can adapt the soil acidity to the plant — this route can mean a lot of work. For the easy-care gardener it is much better to choose a plant with site recommendations which are suitable for the spot we have chosen.

Test with a pH meter available from your garden centre. Nearly all easy-care plants will grow quite happily in mildly acid soil

ACID SOIL

Good points: Acid soil is required for azalea, camellia, blue hydrangea, most heathers, pieris, rhododendron and fine lawn grass.

Bad points: Bacterial and earthworm activity are reduced in distinctly acid soil and many plants suffer under such conditions.
•
Grow acid-loving plants — for others it is necessary to add a dressing of lime if the pH meter indicates very acid soil.

Test with a pH meter available from your garden centre. Nearly all easy-care plants will grow quite happily in mildly alkaline soil

ALKALINE SOIL

Good points: Lime- or chalk-rich soil is satisfactory for carnation, wallflower, delphinium, scabious, cabbage, some shrubs and many alpines.
Bad points: Plant foods are locked up in alkaline soils and the leaves of acid-loving plants such as rhododendron turn yellow.
•
The addition of leaf mould, compost or peat will help to reduce the alkalinity, but avoid plants which require an acid soil.

Feeding

The purpose of a fertilizer is to supply appreciable quantities of one or more of the major plant nutrients — nitrogen, phosphates and potash. Some nutrients are needed only in tiny amounts — these trace elements are contained in the annual application of compost or manure. Feeding plants in the open garden is not vital unless your soil is sandy with little organic matter, but starved plants produce a sub-standard display. The traditional way to feed is to sprinkle a granular fertilizer containing all three major nutrients over the beds and borders in spring and then water on a soluble fertilizer at intervals during summer. This is too much trouble for some easy-care gardeners, and for them a better technique is to use one of the new slow-release fertilizers. One application is made in spring and the plant foods are released over a period of 6 months — the rate of release is controlled by the temperature of the soil.

CHOOSE EASY-CARE PLANTS

Set out here are all the groups of plants which can be grown in the garden. Some of the examples in each type offer a challenge or involve a lot of effort, but there are also easy-care types with some or all of the characteristics listed on page 9.

The Garden Plant Kingdom...

ROSES

Deciduous Shrubs and Trees of the genus Rosa, usually listed separately in the catalogues because of their importance and great popularity

A **Half Standard** is a rose tree with a 2½ ft (75 cm) stem

A **Full Standard** is a rose tree with a 3½ ft (105 cm) stem

WOODY PLANTS

Perennial plants with woody stems which survive the winter

A **Tree** bears only one woody stem at ground level

A **Shrub** bears several woody stems at ground level

A **Climber** has the ability when established to attach itself to or twine around an upright structure. Some weak-stemmed plants which require tying to stakes (e.g climbing roses) are included here

A **Hedge** is a continuous line of Shrubs or Trees in which the individuality of each plant is partly or wholly lost

DECIDUOUS SHRUBS & TREES

Woody plants which shed their leaves in winter

Tree Fruit are Trees which produce edible fruit (e.g apple, pear, peach, plum)

Soft Fruit are Shrubs and Climbers which produce edible fruit (e.g blackcurrant, gooseberry). A few are Herbaceous Plants (e.g strawberry)

EVERGREEN SHRUBS & TREES

Woody plants which retain their leaves during winter

Conifers bear cones and nearly all are Evergreens

Semi-evergreens (e.g privet) retain most of their leaves in a mild winter

TURF PLANTS

Low-growing carpeting plants, nearly always members of the grass family, which can be regularly mown and walked upon

GROUND COVER

Spreading plants which form dense, leafy mats

HERBACEOUS PLANTS

Plants with non-woody stems which generally die down in winter

VEGETABLES

Plants which are grown for their edible roots, stems or leaves. A few are grown for their fruits (e.g tomato, cucumber, marrow, capsicum)

HERBS

Plants which are grown for their medicinal value, their culinary value as garnishes or flavourings, or their cosmetic value as sweet-smelling flowers or leaves

BULBS

Bulbs (more correctly Bulbous Plants) produce underground fleshy organs which are offered for sale for planting indoors or outdoors. Included here are the **True Bulbs, Corms, Rhizomes** and **Tubers**

BIENNIALS

Plants which complete their life span, from seed to death, in two seasons

A **Hardy Biennial** (HB) is sown outdoors in summer, producing stems and leaves in the first season and flowering in the next

Some Perennials are treated as Biennials (e.g wallflower, daisy)

PERENNIALS

Plants which complete their life span, from seed to death, in three or more seasons

A **Hardy Perennial** (HP) will live for years in the garden — the basic plant of the herbaceous border

A **Half-hardy Perennial** (HHP) is not fully hardy and needs to spend its winter in a frost-free place (e.g fuchsia, geranium)

A **Greenhouse Perennial** (GP) is not suitable for outdoor cultivation

A **Rockery Perennial** (RP) is a dwarf Hardy Perennial suitable for growing in a rockery. **Alpine** is an alternative name, although some originated on the shore rather than on mountains, and some delicate True Alpines need to be grown indoors

ANNUALS

Plants which complete their life span, from seed to death, in a single season

A **Hardy Annual** (HA) is sown outdoors in spring

A **Half-hardy Annual** (HHA) cannot withstand frost, and so it is raised under glass and planted outdoors when the danger of frost has passed

A **Greenhouse** (or **Tender**) **Annual** (GA) is too susceptible to cold weather for outdoor cultivation, but may be planted out for a short time in summer

BEDDING PLANTS

Annuals, Biennials or Perennials set out in autumn or spring to provide a temporary display. A **dot plant** is a focal point in a bedding display

In each group of garden plants there are easy-care examples which give good results with a minimum of effort. With some groups (for example Ground Cover) there are lots of easy-care plants — with others such as Tree & Soft Fruit there are only a few easy-care ones. Novelties are interesting, but as a general rule it is better to pick the popular favourites when looking for trees, shrubs, hardy perennials and bedding plants.

...and the Easy-care Types

EVERGREEN SHRUBS & TREES

Evergreen woody plants provide the basic skeleton for the easy-care garden. The leaves provide winter colour (bronze, red, yellow etc as well as green) and there is no annual replanting or cutting back dead growth to ground level each year. Choose the right type — see pages 32–35

GROUND COVER

An excellent choice which should be widely used — see pages 100–101

VEGETABLES

Not really a good idea as a lot of work is involved, but you can grow some quite easily between flowers or shrubs, or in a raised bed

HERBS

Most are easy to grow — see the list on pages 76–77. The problem is to keep rampant growers like mint in check

EASY-CARE FEATURES

- **HARDY** Frost-sensitive plants need winter protection or replacing in spring

- **PERENNIAL** Annuals need replacing every year

- **EVERGREEN** Deciduous shrubs and trees are bare in winter — fallen leaves need raking or sweeping

- **GOOD DISEASE RESISTANCE** Important with roses, asters, some vegetables etc. Check label or textbook

- **PRUNING NOT VITAL** Choose shrubs which do not need cutting back every year — see page 31

- **STAKING NOT NECESSARY** Staking herbaceous border plants can be a chore — choose self-supporting types wherever possible

- **SLOW GROWTH HABIT** Plants which spread very rapidly often call for annual cutting back after a few years

ROSES

Roses are a delight, but the disease-prone ones need regular spraying to keep mildew and black spot at bay. Choose instead an easy-care shrub rose or a modern one with good disease resistance

DECIDUOUS SHRUBS & TREES

Most of the beautiful flowering shrubs lose their leaves in winter, but still play a very important role in the easy-care garden. Many are recommended (see pages 32–33), but few fruit trees and bushes have a place here

TURF PLANTS

If starting from seed look for one of the new slow-growing varieties

BULBS

Choose types which can be left in the ground year after year. This still leaves a large range from which to make your choice — see pages 62–63

BIENNIALS

This small group suffer the same drawback as annuals — they have a limited life span. A few perennials such as foxgloves and hollyhocks are grown as biennials, but the best known ones are wallflowers — grow in clumps between other plants rather than in rows as part of a bedding scheme

BEDDING PLANTS

Massed planting involves too much work — see pages 51–59

ANNUALS

The traditional way of growing annuals is to bed out half-hardy annuals when the risk of frost has gone and then lift them out in late autumn. Containers can be used if you choose with care (see page 56) but formal beds of annuals have no place in the easy-care garden. Put annuals among other plants in a mixed border. The easiest way to grow annuals is to sprinkle seed lightly over the chosen area or to push large seeds of hardy annuals into the soil in spring

PERENNIALS

The herbaceous border was once the most important feature in the traditional garden, but it is not any longer. Constant care is needed. Staking, dead-heading, cutting back in autumn — and during winter it presents a dull and lifeless scene. The best place for hardy perennials is in a mixed border so that when they are dormant there are bulbs and evergreens to provide colour. Recommended perennials are listed on pages 48–49 — the easy-care features include no staking, good disease resistance and no need to lift and divide every couple of years

Planting

You will never finish stocking your garden as long as you are a gardener, so it is important to learn the right way to plant. The recommended method depends on the type of planting material, and with both bare-rooted and container-grown plants a planting mixture rather than ordinary soil should be used to fill the hole. Mix together 1 part soil with 1 part peat and store in a shed until required.

LIFTED PLANTS

There are times when you will have to rely on lifted plants such as perennials dug up at the nursery, bedding plants grown in trays or vegetables moved from a nursery bed. Evergreens are often sold as balled plants — the soil ball is tightly wrapped with netting or polythene sheeting after lifting.

Choose a day when the soil is moist. Squeeze a handful of the soil — it should be wet enough to form a ball and yet dry enough to shatter when dropped on a hard surface

Prepare plants for the move. Always water plants prior to lifting — dry soil would fall away from the roots. Do all you can to keep the soil ball intact

(4) Plant properly. For small plants, fill around the soil ball with loose soil and firm with the fingers or the trowel handle. With larger plants, fine soil should be added, each layer being gently compressed with the fists until the hole is full. Stake trees at planting time. Handle non-woody plants by the soil ball or the leaves — never by the stem. Water in after planting

(3) Plant at the right depth. Set all bedding plants, seedlings and rooted cuttings so that the top of the soil ball is just below ground level. With lifted mature plants use the old soil mark on the stems as your guide

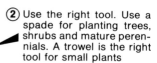

(2) Use the right tool. Use a spade for planting trees, shrubs and mature perennials. A trowel is the right tool for small plants

(1) Dig the hole to fit the roots. The hole should be much wider than it is deep — the roots at the base and at the side should never have to be bent to fit into the hole

BARE-ROOTED PLANTS

Bare-rooted plants are dug up at the nursery and transported without soil — once all roses were bought this way. Damp material such as peat is packed around the roots to prevent drying out. Bare-rooted plants are less expensive than their container-grown counterparts but it is not true that they are always more difficult to establish. Some shrubs actually root more easily.

Planting time is the dormant season between autumn and spring — choose mid October–late November if you can, but delay planting until March if the soil is heavy and wet. Cut off leaves, dead flowers, weak stems and damaged roots. If the stem is shrivelled plunge the roots in a bucket of water for 2 hours before planting

(3) Work a couple of trowelfuls of the planting mixture around the roots. Shake the plant gently up and down — add a little more planting mixture. Firm this around the roots with the fists — do not press too hard. Half-fill the hole with more planting mixture and firm it down

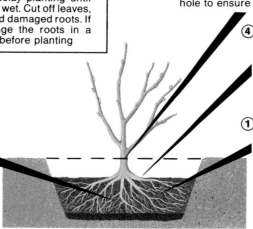

(2) The old soil mark should be level with the soil surface — set a board across the top of the hole to ensure correct planting depth

(4) Add more planting mixture until the hole is full. Firm by pressing with the fists or gentle treading — on no account tread heavily. Loosen the surface once the hole has been filled. Water in after planting

(1) The hole should be wide enough to allow the roots to be spread evenly. Put a layer of planting mixture (see above) at the bottom of the hole — important if soil condition is poor

CONTAINER-GROWN PLANTS

The quickest way to obtain instant colour and greenery is to use container-grown plants — root disturbance is avoided. A container-grown plant will have been raised as a seedling, cutting or grafted rootstock and then potted on until housed in a whalehide, plastic or metal container. Pot-grown plants are miniature versions.

A large container-grown plant should *not* have been lifted from the open ground and its roots and surrounding soil stuffed into the container prior to sale. The test is to pull the plant gently and see if the soil ball comes up easily. If it does, the plant should be rejected. Planting can take place at any time of the year, but the soil must be neither frozen nor waterlogged

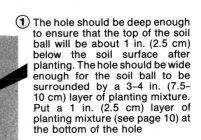

② Water the container thoroughly. Cut down the side of the container when it is stood in the hole. Remove the cover and its base very carefully — do not disturb the soil ball. Water about an hour before planting. Place your hand around the crown of the plant and turn the container over. Gently remove — tap the sides with a trowel if necessary

④ After planting there should be a shallow water-holding basin. Water in after planting

③ Examine the exposed surface — cut away circling or tangled roots but do not break up the soil ball. Fill the space between the soil ball and the sides of the hole with planting mixture. Firm down the planting mixture with your hands

① The hole should be deep enough to ensure that the top of the soil ball will be about 1 in. (2.5 cm) below the soil surface after planting. The hole should be wide enough for the soil ball to be surrounded by a 3–4 in. (7.5–10 cm) layer of planting mixture. Put a 1 in. (2.5 cm) layer of planting mixture (see page 10) at the bottom of the hole

PUT GROUND COVER AROUND THE PLANTS

Ground cover around the plants is the third cornerstone of easy-care gardening. Leaving the soil uncovered will inevitably lead to a weed problem — walking on uncovered soil will often lead to a surface capping problem. Ground cover is the answer. This may be a humus mulch (page 96) to improve the soil and cut down the need to weed and water, a weed control mulch (page 99) to eliminate weeds or the use of ground cover plants (page 100) to improve appearance and inhibit the germination of weed seeds.

Humus mulch

Weed control mulch

Ground cover plants

CREATE AN EASY-CARE DESIGN

Articles and books on garden design show you how to create an attractive garden with a professional look. You will find a number of basic rules. Draw a scale plan. Aim for something between the over-plain and the over-fussy. Create points of interest, plant a mixture of evergreens and deciduous types, hide eyesores and so on. Here design is covered from a different angle — the way to arrange the garden so that maintenance work is reduced to a minimum. Easy-care designs have one feature in common — hard (non-living) landscaping is important and soft landscaping (the use of plants) avoids types which need lifting every year. However, don't be slavish about these things — of course you should put in showy tulips every year if these are a favourite feature, but remember it will mean a bit of extra work.

Styles

FORMAL GARDEN

This is the style which surrounds millions of suburban homes. The back garden is dominated by the lawn, and this is flanked and sometimes perforated by beds and borders filled with flowers and roses. There is often an allotment-style vegetable plot and the beds have neat straight, round or oval lines. Shrubs are now more often planted than they used to be, but annuals and hardy perennials are usually dominant.

COTTAGE GARDEN

A lovely part of the rural scene. There is no clear design — flowers are crowded together and new introductions are planted wherever there is room. Pots and old sinks, narrow paths and brick walls form the framework for annuals, perennials, roses, some shrubs, vegetables etc. Despite the 'natural' look it is not an easy-care style — without regular cutting-back, dead-heading, watering etc it can look a mess.

INFORMAL GARDEN

This is the basic easy-care style. Hard landscaping provides weed-free paths, patio, raised beds etc. The beds and borders around the lawn are filled with a mixture of evergreen and deciduous trees and shrubs which have a good trouble-free reputation. Between these woody plants a selection of bulbs, hardy perennials and perhaps some annuals are grown. The final feature is ground cover between these plants.

ARCHITECTURAL GARDEN

Another type of easy-care garden, but here the hard landscaping is dominant. Stone, water, brick, containers, gravel etc take centre stage and are chosen for their decorative qualities. Plants are introduced to add living colour and living shapes. A good example is the small front garden in which the grass has been removed and replaced by gravel or paving on which raised beds are built or containers are stood.

Hard Landscaping

The proper use of hard (that is, non-living) materials can reduce the maintenance work you have to do in the garden. You will find numerous examples on later pages — the building of raised beds for vegetables, the introduction of mowing strips around the lawn, the replacement of grass paths by reconstituted stone ones etc. A few words of warning. Hard landscaping is hard work — don't even think about doing it yourself if the effort is going to be more than you are used to. Even if you are fit and strong you must know what you are doing — read a manual or enrol a skilled friend before putting in foundations. Finally, make sure that the colour and material are in keeping with the house.

SURFACING MATERIALS

BRICKS & BLOCKS		No heavy lifting is necessary. Bricks make an excellent path where an old-world look is required. Don't use ordinary bricks — ask for paving ones. As an alternative you can use brick-like blocks (paviors) made of clay or concrete
STONE & SLABS		Natural stone gives an air of luxury, but slate, sandstone, yorkstone etc are very expensive. Slabs made of concrete or reconstituted stone are a much more popular and inexpensive alternative these days
MACADAM		This mixture of stone chippings with tar or bitumen is the favourite material for drives and has several names — asphalt, black top, 'Tarmac' etc. This is not a job for an amateur — choose your contractor with care
CRAZY PAVING		Laying flagstones or paving slabs can be heavy work and you generally have to keep to straight lines — with crazy paving the pieces are smaller and the informal effect means that you don't have to aim for a perfect fit
CONCRETE		Concrete is criticised by many for its austere look, but it remains a popular material for both paths and drives. It is durable, fairly inexpensive and suitable for curving or irregular pathways. Laying concrete is for the fit, strong and knowledgeable
WOOD & BARK		Pulverised or shredded bark has become a popular material for paths in woodland and wild gardens. It is soft underfoot but requires topping up every few years. Sawn log rounds are sometimes set in the shredded bark
GRAVEL & PEBBLES		Gravel is by far the cheapest material. Shingle (small stones smoothed by water) and true gravel (stone chips from a quarry) are the types available. Large rounded pebbles are sometimes used for small decorative areas
PATTERN-PRINTED CONCRETE		A post-war development for paths, drives and patios. A concrete-based mix is poured over the area and a roller is taken over the surface before it has set. The roller leaves an embossed pattern in the form of blocks, slabs or crazy paving

CONSTRUCTIONAL MATERIALS

BRICKS

Bricks are excellent for building retaining walls, steps etc — choose either an engineering or a facing brick. A solid foundation of hardcore and rubble is needed — do not build a wall over 4 ft (1.2 m) high unless you are experienced

STONE

Many types of stone can be used for walling — limestone, slate, granite, sandstone etc. The usual pattern is a random one with irregular blocks placed on top of each other. The cost and work involved make it impractical

BLOCKS

Reconstituted stone blocks have become the favourite material for garden walling. They generally have a textured face and various shapes and sizes can be obtained. Other types include solid concrete blocks and pierced screen blocks

WOOD

Wood has many constructional uses — fencing, pergolas, trellis, buildings, screens, furniture etc. Railway sleepers can be used for raised beds. Never use softwood unless it has been properly treated with a preservative

FEATURES TO REDUCE...

LAWN

... edges which cannot be cut by the mower, and so need cutting with shears or a strimmer

... a small and perhaps shady lawn by removing it altogether and replacing it with a paved or gravel area if you are not devoted to grass

... the number of beds, trees, containers etc in the grass

BEDS & BORDERS

... wide borders which have to be walked on to reach plants at the back

... beds used for planting out annuals in formal designs

... herbaceous borders — they involve a lot of work and look bare and unsightly for part of the year

PLANTS

... bedding plants except as fillers in borders or in containers

... hardy perennials, especially those which need staking

... tulips, gladioli etc and other bulbs which need lifting every year

... vegetables

... soft fruit

... vigorous fruit trees

SOIL

... annual digging — after initial cultivation a bed or border should be kept in condition by using an organic dressing

... bare ground — cover with a mulch or ground cover plants to keep down weeds

DESIGN

... the area devoted to the rock garden. If you don't have a rockery grow alpines in a trough or raised bed

... high hedges — low hedges are much easier to cut

... an allotment-type vegetable plot — it is much easier to grow vegetables in beds surrounded by gravel or bark

... the use of small containers scattered about the garden

... the use of moss-lined hanging baskets

MAINTENANCE

... watering lawns in dry weather — save the water for annuals and newly-planted trees and shrubs

... having to hack back overgrown shrubs by choosing wisely and planting at the recommended spacings

FEATURES TO INCREASE...

LAWN

... the use of mowing or edging strips

... the height of the cut if it is less than 1 in. (2.5 cm)

... curved corners rather than right-angled ones

... the area of rough grassland with trees and naturalised bulbs if the garden is large

BEDS & BORDERS

... mulching or the use of ground cover plants over areas of bare ground

... the erection of raised beds in which all the plants can be reached without stepping on the surface

... the use of narrow beds instead of open ground with long rows of plants in the vegetable garden

PLANTS

... the planting of shrubs, especially those which do not need hard pruning

... the planting of those bulbs which do not need lifting every year

... the planting of those roses which do not need spraying

... the planting of evergreens, but do grow some deciduous (leaf-losing) shrubs for contrast and extra interest

... the use of ground cover plants

... the use of drought-resistant plants

SOIL

... the area of soil covered by ground cover plants or a mulch

... the use of season-long slow-release fertilizers rather than soluble ones which need regular application

DESIGN

... the use of fences with or without climbing plants in place of hedges which need trimming

... paths of slabs, bricks or gravel instead of grass ones

... the use of self-watering hanging baskets instead of free-draining ones

MAINTENANCE

... the use of selective weed-killers instead of hand pulling to get rid of perennial weeds

... the use of easy-care aids such as grabbers, strimmers, tip bags etc

... automation — automatic ventilators and automatic watering in a greenhouse need not be expensive

... the use of underground irrigation in the garden if you can afford it

THE LAWN

For generations the lawn has been the centrepiece of most gardens. In both small and large plots the area of grass has traditionally been the place where deckchairs were opened, children played their games and adults laid in the sun. Nowadays the patio next to the house has become the outdoor living area for many people, but the lawn still retains its unique charm.

A delight perhaps, but a 'bowling green' lawn made up of fine-leaved grasses has no place in the work-saving garden. It is hard to create and even harder to maintain in good condition. You will need to follow a regular routine of feeding, weeding, aerating, top dressing, edging and so on as well as cutting every few days between spring and autumn. A utility lawn made up of broader-leaved grasses is much easier to care for and is more tolerant of hard wear and occasional neglect.

On the following pages of this chapter you will discover the various ways in which you can cut down the amount of time you need to spend on caring for your lawn. There is no way, however, of avoiding the need to mow regularly and also to carry out occasional maintenance work. This is one of the reasons why some garden designers have started to question the wisdom of having a lawn when the garden is very small.

The point they make is that a tiny patch of grass at the front of a terrace or semi-detached house is not often an attractive feature and is not worth the effort involved. In their view it is better to put the area down to 'hard' landscaping (gravel or stone paving) between borders, raised beds and/or containers filled with shrubs and flowers.

This approach may be too extreme. The small lawn *can* be an attractive feature and it need not be difficult to care for, provided it satisfies certain conditions. It should not be in dense shade — moss control here is impossible. It should also be easily accessible for the mower — carrying equipment from the shed in the back garden to the plot in the front each week can be a hard and irritating task.

So size alone should not be the reason for getting rid of your lawn. The decision should be based on whether an attractive area of grass can be maintained without a great deal of effort on the site in question. A front garden made up of gravel or paving may look fine in summer when the pots and beds are filled with flowers, but in winter we seem to need that patch of living green to remind us that not all is dead in the garden.

LAWN TYPE

The **LUXURY LAWN** has a velvety look. Two factors are responsible for this appearance — the turf is made up of Bent and Fescue grasses which have very narrow leaves and the lawn is mown at frequent intervals (twice a week in summer) so that it is kept at a height of ½ in. (1 cm). The beauty of a first rate Luxury Lawn is unmatched by any other type but it has too many drawbacks for the gardener with little time to spare. Seed and turf are more expensive than for a Utility Lawn and establishment from seed takes a long time. In addition the Luxury Lawn will not stand up to heavy wear and it quickly deteriorates if there is a period of neglect.

The **UTILITY LAWN** has a lush and low-growing leafy look. It is a pleasure to see and walk on when well-grown — this is the lawn for you. It is *not* a second-rate Luxury Lawn — it is a different type of turf with its own merits and appeal. The basic difference from its closely-cut sister is that it is the broad-leaved lawn grasses which are dominant. This means that the native coarse grasses which invade lawns are hidden, but they would stand out as weeds in a Luxury Lawn. The velvet look is missing, but you can easily create a striped effect by using a mower with a roller. If you are starting from scratch with seed, choose a mixture which is described as slow growing.

The **ROUGH LAWN** has a natural look. The grass is allowed to grow about 3–4 in. (7.5–10 cm) high and the place for this type of grassland is in the semi-wild areas on the fringes of a large garden. Here is the place where bulbs can be naturalised and left to die down after they have bloomed. The first cut is made when the bulb foliage has withered away in spring and then the grass is mown every 2–3 weeks until October. A useful technique is to mow a strip at weekly intervals through this area of Rough Lawn so as to create a Utility Lawn path which leads to various points of interest within the 'natural' part of the garden. When starting from scratch use a Ryegrass seed mixture or meadow turf.

The **WILDFLOWER MEADOW** has a colourful look. A mixture of fine-leaved grasses is sown in infertile but free-draining soil and a selection of wildflower seeds is sown at the same time. Cutting is an occasional rather than a regular task and there are no hard-and-fast rules. A popular maintenance plan for an established Wildflower Meadow is to make the first cut when the spring flowers have died down and then repeat the mowing about a month later. The final cut is made in September. It all sounds so simple and desirable, but there are problems. Scything is necessary if your mower will not cut at 3–4 in. (7.5–10 cm), and the 'flowery meadow' so often turns into a weed-ridden untidy eyesore.

LAWN SHAPE & DESIGN

The Golden Rule

Don't let your lawn be an obstacle course for the mower. An area of grass strewn with isolated trees, island beds, narrow paths and items of furniture can take twice as long to cut as a well-designed lawn.

Round off sharp corners and smooth out tight curves — the outline should ideally be roughly oval or kidney-shaped. Grass paths and the strips between island beds and the edge of the lawn should be at least 3 ft (1 m) wide.

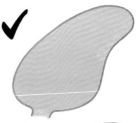

Avoid having a scatter of trees, shrubs and beds over the grass — they make the lawn look smaller and mowing becomes a long and tedious process. If it is possible group at least some of the plants together into a single large bed.

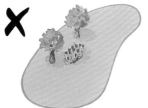

If there are one or more trees already on the lawn do cut off the lower branches if they interfere with easy mowing. If you are planning to put in a tree then choose a spot elsewhere in the garden or at the side of the lawn.

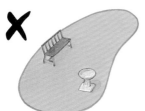

Seats, pots, sundials etc are attractive features in a garden but they do not belong on the lawn if you want mowing to be as easy a task as possible. Site furniture elsewhere in the garden or on paving along the lawn edge.

Spring bulbs in flower are always a welcome sight but they should not be planted in a luxury or utility lawn. The grass cannot be cut for 6 weeks after the blooms have faded, so naturalise Narcissi etc in rough grassland.

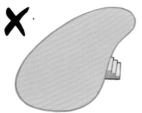

Avoid restricted access to the lawn. If there is just one narrow entry point then excessive wear and bare patches are inevitable, and that means some reseeding or returfing. Make sure that the mower can be moved easily on and off the lawn.

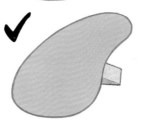

CHOOSING A MOWER

For nearly all gardeners cutting the lawn is the one big job which has to be done every week during the growing season. Once this meant the tiring task of pushing a hand mower, but nowadays there is a vast range of power models to suit every pocket. There are hundreds of types from which to make your choice and you will have to consider several different factors if you are going to find the right one for your particular patch.

Types of Power

ELECTRICITY

Most mowers these days are driven by electricity. Lightweight models are inexpensive and they do a good job on a small lawn. In addition to being generally more compact than petrol-driven models they are also quieter and easier to maintain. There are several drawbacks — the electric model is not for the larger lawn as 200 ft (60 m) of cable is about the maximum length. Petrol is needed for larger and more powerful engines on wide-cut machines, and an electric model may overheat if used on rough grass over a large area. Rules concerning plug type, use on wet grass and the need for a residual circuit breaker must be followed.

PETROL

This power source is independent of the house supply and so there is no cable to move and any size of lawn can be cut. Engines capable of cutting wide swathes and dealing with tall grass are practical, but these mowers are more complex and so are more expensive and heavier than electric models. Regular maintenance and annual servicing are essential and this power source has to be bought and stored.

Width of Cut

Size of lawn		Recommended minimum cutting width
Small lawn:	less than 500 sq.ft (less than 45 sq.m)	10-12 in. (25-30 cm)
Average lawn:	500-2000 sq.ft (45-180 sq.m)	12-14 in. (30-35 cm)
Large lawn:	over 2000 sq.ft (over 180 sq.m)	14-18 in. (35-45 cm)

A Word of Warning

Where money is no object you may be tempted to buy a mower which is much heavier and wider than the recommended minimum. Take care — an oversized machine on a small awkwardly-shaped lawn will make mowing more and not less time-consuming.

Types of Mower

CYLINDER

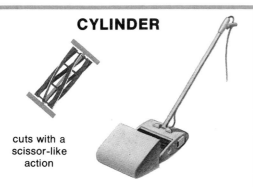

cuts with a scissor-like action

Rollers or a combination of wheels and roller support the machine above the lawn — a series of spiral blades on a horizontal shaft rotate at high speed against a bottom fixed blade to cut the grass. Both the electric and petrol models are powered versions of the traditional hand-driven mower. The cylinder arrangement gives the finest and closest cut of all, but careful setting is essential and it will not cut wet grass or wiry grass stalks. Bumpy lawns may be scalped and these machines are generally more expensive than rotary models with the same cutting width. The quality of the cut is determined by the number of blades on the cylinder — 5 is the usual number but 8–12 are needed for a bowling green effect. The large petrol version should only be chosen if the grass area is extensive and you want a luxury-grade lawn.

ROTARY

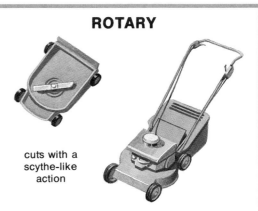

cuts with a scythe-like action

Wheels or wheels plus a roller support the machine above the lawn — under the cover the horizontal blade or blades rotate at high speed to cut the grass. Both electric and petrol models are available. Choose the lightweight electric one only if the lawn is small — for a larger area you will need the self-propelled petrol model where both wheels as well as blades are driven by the motor. The quality of cut is not as good as a cylinder, but it is better for uneven lawns, wet grass and long turf. A rear-mounted grass box is usually present.

RIDE-ON

This type of mower is worth considering if you have an acre or more to care for. The most popular version is the 4-wheeled tractor with a rotary mower fitted between the wheels. Most people find that mowing suddenly becomes enjoyable, but such mowers are expensive, difficult to use in awkward corners and can cause compaction on heavy land in wet weather.

HOVER

cuts with a scythe-like action

A fan beneath the canopy builds up an air cushion on which the machine floats — under the cover the horizontal blade rotates at high speed to cut the grass. The 12 in. (30 cm) electric model is very popular — the hovers are easier to move over the lawn than any other mower type. It deals easily with awkward corners, bumpy turf etc and is easily stored. The petrol version is heavier and noisier, and is less popular. The drawbacks are that with most models the clippings are thrown about and it is difficult to mow in straight lines.

USING THE MOWER

The Golden Rule

The purpose of mowing a utility lawn is to keep the grass tall enough to ensure vigorous root activity but short enough for it to be attractive to the observer. The height of the grass should not vary a great deal during the growing season.

Mowing does much more than merely keeping the lawn looking attractive. When the grass is cut regularly but not too closely, the development of excessive leaf growth is prevented. The result is that the loss of nutrients is cut down and the menace of weeds, worms and unwanted grasses is reduced. The lawn grasses develop a dwarf habit and the production of tillers is stimulated. It is the growth of these side-shoots which thickens the turf in summer.

The Basics

START

Begin in **March** or **early April**, depending on the locality and the weather. It is time for the first cut when the soil is reasonably dry and the grass is starting to grow actively. With this first cut set the blades high so that the grass is merely tipped, not shorn.

MARCH

MOW REGULARLY

As a general rule the cutting height should be 1 in. (2.5 cm) and mowing should take place at weekly intervals. However, there are several exceptions to this standard procedure:

- Set the blades at 1¼–1½ in. (3–4 cm) for the first couple of cuts in spring and for the last few cuts in autumn.
- Set the blades at 1½ in. (4 cm) during periods of prolonged drought if the lawn is not being regularly watered. The longer grass will help to cut down water loss.
- Cut at fortnightly rather than weekly intervals if the grass is growing very slowly — for example under trees or during prolonged drought.
- If you have had to be away for a couple of weeks or more in summer then merely tip it at the first cut following your return. Reduce the height at the next cut and then continue with 1 in. (2.5 cm) high cuts.

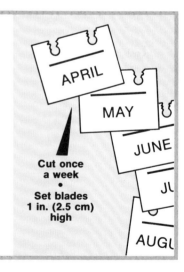

APRIL

MAY

JUNE

JU

AUGU

Cut once a week
•
Set blades 1 in. (2.5 cm) high

FINISH

Stop in **October** when the growth of the grass has slowed right down and the soil has become very moist. Put the mower away, but rake off fallen leaves on the surface of the lawn. Keen gardeners lightly 'top' the grass occasionally in winter when the weather is mild, but it is not essential. Avoid walking on the lawn when it is frozen or covered in snow.

OCTOBER

Before you Start

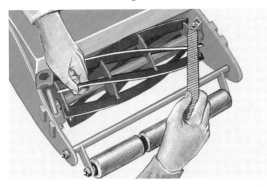

Before the first cut of the season it is essential to check that the mower is in good running order and the blades are sharp — read the manual for instructions. Make sure all faults are repaired before the grass starts to grow.

Set the blades at the recommended height — look in the manufacturer's instruction book for the method of changing the height of cut. Make sure that both sides of a cylinder mower are set at the same height. With a petrol-powered mower fill up with sufficient fuel before you start. Make sure that the lawn surface is clear of objects which could damage the blades — stones, bones, toys etc. Never cut if there is frost on the lawn.

After you Finish

Remove all clippings and caked earth with a rag and stiff brush — pay particular attention to blades, rollers, cylinders and the canopy under a rotary or hover mower. This may seem like more work — but it will save the frustration of a disappointing or slow cutting action. Correct storage is essential — there should be no chance of rain or dripping water reaching the machine. At the end of the season oil and clean as instructed in the manual. Get the machine serviced if it is not in good condition. Book this service in autumn or winter — do not wait until spring.

Leave off the Grass Box

Most textbooks will tell you to use a grass box if one is available so that the grass clippings can be removed each time you mow. The appearance of the lawn is improved, the danger of spreading weeds is reduced and there is less chance of building up a spongy layer of dead grass ('thatch'). There is another side to the story. Leaving short clippings on the surface returns some of the nutrients to the soil so that feeding is much less necessary, and the baking effect of the sun is reduced during dry spells in summer. Most important of all is the fact that not using a grass box means that you do not have to stop at regular intervals to empty it and then have to dispose of the clippings when mowing is over.

A Word of Warning

Busy gardeners sometimes try to save time by cutting the grass at the lowest setting the mower will allow in the belief that they can then wait for at least a couple of weeks before another scalping will be necessary. This technique is almost guaranteed to ruin the lawn. The sudden loss of such a large quantity of leaf shocks the grass so that its vigour is reduced. The thin and open turf which results is soon invaded by moss, pearlwort, yarrow and other weeds.

The Striped Effect

A striped effect is sometimes regarded as a sign of a healthy and cared-for lawn, but it is nothing of the sort. It merely results from cutting the grass in parallel strips with a mower which is fitted with a roller. The alternate stripes are mown in opposite directions, and stripes are useful for masking small imperfections and colour variations. This is a technique for good drivers — it is unsightly if it is not done neatly and accurately.

TRIMMING THE EDGES

The Golden Rule

Mowing regularly is vital, but trimming the edges is an extra task and is not essential every time you cut the grass. In fact it is not necessary at all in the lawn designed for low maintenance. Installing mowing strips is the answer.

Horizontal Trimming

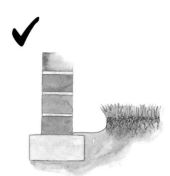

There may be several places where the mower cannot reach, such as around trees, along walls and under large shrubs. For long grass in these areas you will need a horizontal trimmer, and by far the best choice is an electric strimmer which cuts by means of a replaceable nylon cord — using long-handled shears is a laborious job if the area is large. In nearly all situations this need to trim can be eliminated by leaving a space between the grass and the obstacle — see below for details.

Vertical Trimming

Vertical trimming, or edging, is the removal of grass from the edge of the lawn to give a neat appearance. The traditional method is to use a half-moon edging iron at the start of the season, cutting along a plank of wood to give a straight edge. Then, after each mowing an edging tool is used to trim the grass left by the mower. Ordinary hand shears are not suitable — long-handled edging shears can be used but few people enjoy this back-aching job. A variety of power-driven tools is available — strimmers, electric edgers etc, but all involve an extra job after mowing. Do consider doing away with the need for edging by installing a **mowing strip**. This consists of a line of slabs, bricks, tiles or blocks between the lawn edge and the path, bed, border or wall. The top of this mowing strip is set slightly below the surface of the turf so that the mower can be taken over the top of the hard surface. For a perfect job the slabs should be fixed with blobs of mortar on to a foundation of compacted sand, but this is not vital.

Edging Strips

Instead of using a mowing strip a narrow trench is sometimes left around the lawn. This uncovered trench can allow the mower to go over the edge, but it is usually necessary to install an edging strip as shown.

The top of the strip should be below the soil surface so that the lawn mower can pass over the edge

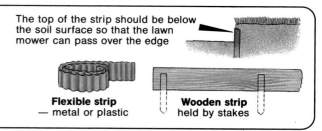

Flexible strip — metal or plastic

Wooden strip held by stakes

LOOKING AFTER THE LAWN

The Golden Rule

If the lawn is your pride and joy then you will have to carry out a number of maintenance jobs during the year. In the work-saving garden restrict yourself to those tasks which are really vital as detailed below.

Feeding

Every gardening textbook with a chapter on lawns will tell you to feed the grass with fertilizer at least once a year. This must seem strange advice for people who want to spend less time tending to their lawns. The purpose of feeding is to make the grass grow more quickly, and they want the grass to grow more slowly! Actually it is good advice, as feeding does more than make the grass grow more quickly. It also builds up the density of the grass covering the surface and the resistance of the turf to drought and disease. Weeds and moss find it more difficult to get a foothold in closely-knit turf. Where time or money shortage makes an annual feeding programme difficult you should follow the guide on the right.

Look at the grass in early autumn and find the most appropriate description for the turf. Carry out the recommended treatment.

- **The surface is green and the grass is reasonably thick and dense.**
  A nitrogen-rich fertilizer next spring would be beneficial, but it can be omitted if the grass clippings are left on the lawn.

- **The surface is pale green and the grass is sparse over part or all of the lawn.**
  Apply a fertilizer next spring. Use a powder or granular formulation through a distributor in late April or May — you can hire one of these wheeled machines. Use a combined 'weed-and-feed' product if weeds are a serious problem. Choose a day when the grass is dry and the soil is moist.

Watering

During a period of drought there is at first a loss of springiness in the turf and a general dullness over the surface. Later on the grass turns straw-coloured and unsightly. You will have to choose between two courses of action. First, you can decide to leave it to nature. Lawn grasses are very rarely killed by drought and recover quite quickly once the rains return. Furthermore, water is often banned for garden use in times of prolonged drought. The problem with leaving it to nature is that drought-resistant weeds such as yarrow and clover can spread rapidly and the lawn has a mottled appearance for some time once the drought is over. So watering is the alternative course of action, but it must be thorough. This calls for applying at least 4 gallons per 10 sq.ft (20 litres per sq.m) once a week until the dry spell ends. Do not use a watering can or a hosepipe propped on the handle of a spade — water with either a rotary or oscillating sprinkler so that a large area is covered. Do not try to take a middle course of action by sprinkling every few days to dampen the surface — this will do more harm than good.

ROTARY SPRINKLER

Rotating arms produce a circle of fine droplets. Very popular and many brands are available. Some are adjustable for area covered

OSCILLATING SPRINKLER

A horizontal tube bearing a series of fine holes slowly turns from side to side. A rectangular spray pattern is obtained — all are adjustable for area covered

Scarifying and Aerating

Scarifying means taking up debris and dead grass with a rake or rake-like implement — aerating means making holes or slits in the surface. As a low-maintenance gardener you may not want to bother with these techniques — if you do then remember to do the work in autumn and not in spring. You can hire a power-driven rake or aerator.

Weed Control

It is inevitable that some weeds will appear in your lawn and as a labour-saving gardener you will have to accept their presence. The enthusiast gets to work with repeat treatments using a hormone preparation in spring, but for the regularly-cut utility lawn it should only be necessary to take serious action when weeds get out of hand. This three-part programme should keep them under control:

- Learn to live with scattered clumps of daisies, buttercups, clover, etc. Their leaves are reasonably small and should not be too unsightly.
- A few weeds make large rosettes which do stand out — examples include plantains, thistles and dandelions. Grub these out with an old knife, apple corer, daisy grubber or narrow trowel.
- Patches of small-leaved weeds can be dealt with by spot-treating with a ready-to-use hormone preparation or a sprinkle of a weed-and-feed product or lawn sand.

If weeds are beginning to take over it is worth considering using an overall treatment. This can be a weed-and-feed formulation through a distributor (see page 25) or a diluted hormone spray through a watering can. These hormones are taken in by the leaves and go down to the roots — more than one treatment may be necessary. Lawn sand is different — it burns off the leaves and can scorch the grass if you fail to follow the directions carefully.

KEY

1 Grub out root with a knife or small trowel

2 Spot-treat with a hormone preparation — 1 treatment is often sufficient

3 Spot-treat with a hormone preparation — 2 or more treatments will be necessary

4 Spot-treat with lawn sand

5 No effective chemical treatment available

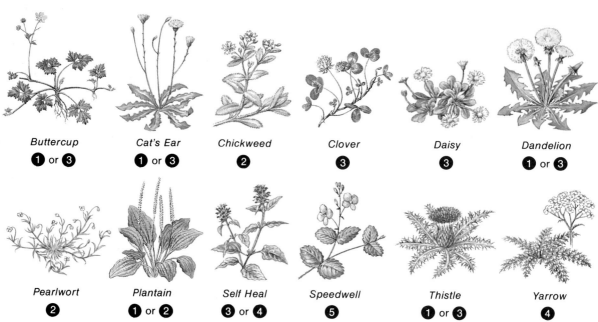

Buttercup
1 or **3**

Cat's Ear
1 or **3**

Chickweed
2

Clover
3

Daisy
3

Dandelion
1 or **3**

Pearlwort
2

Plantain
1 or **2**

Self Heal
3 or **4**

Speedwell
5

Thistle
1 or **3**

Yarrow
4

Moss Control

Small patches of moss are not a problem, but large mossy areas can be unsightly. Unfortunately there is no easy solution. You can burn moss off with lawn sand or obtain longer control with a proprietary moss killer containing dichlorophen, but these offer only short- or medium-term relief. If you don't remove the basic cause or causes then the moss will return. Poor drainage is an important culprit, so making holes with a fork in a mossy patch on compacted soil will help. Other causes are shade, lack of nutrients in sandy soil and over acidity (lime will help but do test first). The best advice is to feed in spring, aerate if you can, and always cut at the recommended height — see page 22.

GRASS SUBSTITUTES

The Golden Rule

There are a number of materials other than grass which can be used to cover the area occupied by your front lawn. The idea of not having to mow every week may sound attractive, but check the disadvantages before removing the turf.

Living Substitutes

Grass is not the only lawn-making plant — Chamomile lawns have been around for hundreds of years. If you want something different and have a well-drained site then you can create one of these lawns by planting seedlings of Anthemis nobilis 'Treneague' at 6 in. (15 cm) intervals in weed-free soil. The Thyme lawn (Thymus serpyllum) is more popular, and other plants which are occasionally used are Clover, Moss and Yarrow.

No weekly cutting and with some the promise of ground-hugging flowers and fragrance... but the non-grass lawn has no place in the low-maintenance garden. The surface usually looks ragged, will not stand up to heavy wear and may turn brown in winter. Even worse, grass becomes a common weed for which there is no chemical control. Hand-pulling over a large area is a tedious task... mowing grass is much less tiring.

Perhaps the best plan is to create a non-grass lawn on a small plot away from the main lawn. Bound it by a path or walls as edge trimming is not really practical.

Non-living Substitutes

Your front lawn may be small and shaded by both the house and boundary walls. Poor drainage may be an additional problem and in such a situation the turf will be poor no matter what you do. The trend these days is to remove the grass and cover the surface with a non-living material on which containers filled with plants are stood. This type of 'lawn' is a low-maintenance feature once it has been created, but it does have a serious disadvantage for many people. This drawback is a matter of personal taste — for many the front garden should be a living thing, green in winter and growing (with all its imperfections) in summer.

Only you can decide whether the non-living 'lawn' is for you. Paving stones are the favourite material — a formal pattern with rectangular or square reconstituted stone slabs or an informal design with crazy paving. Gravel is less harsh and is becoming increasingly popular — lay it on heavy duty perforated polyethylene sheeting which has been placed over level and compacted ground.

Beds or borders can be left around or within this hard landscaping, or you can cover the whole area and place tubs, urns, troughs etc on the surface. Paving stones and gravel are not the only materials which can be used as a non-living substitute for grass — shredded bark is occasionally used to provide a 'natural' look and synthetic turf made of plastic is available but has never become popular for home gardens.

CHAPTER 4

SHRUBS & TREES

In most gardens shrubs (and to a lesser extent trees, conifers and climbers) have a vital role to play. Bulbs, roses, bedding plants, border perennials etc provide colour from spring to autumn, but in the depths of winter we must rely on evergreen or winter-flowering trees and shrubs to provide most of the interest in the garden. Even more important is the fact that the woody plants give the living part of the garden its shape — they provide the skeleton which rises above the other plants.

The list of virtues does not end there. Shrubs and trees bring an air of maturity and they can also be used to increase privacy, act as wind breaks, cut down the weed problem and screen out unsightly objects. It is no wonder that the popularity of these plants has greatly increased in recent years.

For the gardener who wants to save work there is an additional virtue — trees and shrubs are much less trouble than annuals, vegetables, lawns, fruit and the herbaceous border. Once fully established there is little work to be done — no constant feeding or spraying, no regular dead-heading and staking, no annual replanting or sowing ritual and no rushing out with the watering can or hosepipe every time the weather turns dry.

This labour-saving aspect of woody plants is well-known and you will find it mentioned in the textbooks, but there is a drawback which is not often raised. Trees, conifers and large shrubs are expensive compared with border perennials, bedding plants and packets of seed, so you should follow the rules for success carefully — you will find them in this chapter. The basic rule to remember is that various shrubs, conifers, climbers and so on laid out for you at the garden centre differ widely in their requirements, reliability, ease of cultivation and height at maturity. The first step, therefore, is to choose wisely. Some shrubs can be quite a lot of work and can be a challenge to grow — others are trouble-free and as tough as weeds. Having made your choice it is essential that the specimens you have bought should be planted properly. You will probably have selected container-grown plants rather than bare-rooted ones which have to be put in during the cold months of the year, but do not regard container planting as 'easy'. Follow the rules laid down in Chapter 2. Equally important is the need to leave enough space between the plants — see page 36. The final point concerns pruning, and this should not worry you. By choosing easy-care varieties and by not planting too closely this mysterious task becomes a simple or unnecessary job — see page 37.

CHOOSE EASY-CARE TYPES

The Basic Groups

SHRUB

A shrub is a perennial plant which bears several woody stems at ground level. A mature shrub may be only a few inches high or as tall as 20 ft (6 m), depending on variety. The most popular group — you can have flowers during every month of the year by planting quite a modest selection. Bought primarily to provide attractive foliage and/or flowers, and the shape is often of secondary importance.

Framework Shrub: 6 ft (1.8 m) or over — use as a focal point or with others to provide the framework of the shrub or mixed border.

Fill-in Shrub: 1½–6 ft (45 cm–1.8 m) — most shrubs belong here. In a small garden use as framework plants — in a large garden they can be used as ground cover under trees and large shrubs.

Ground-cover Shrub: under 1½ ft (45 cm) — wide-spreading and low-growing. Use as a weed-smothering blanket for covering bare ground.

Several shrubs, such as Pyracantha, Winter Jasmine and Kerria, are not true climbers but are commonly grown against walls and trellis-work.

The dividing line between trees and shrubs is not always clear-cut. Several shrubs, such as Holly, Dogwood and Hazel, may grow as small trees.

CLIMBER

A climber is a perennial plant which has the ability to attach itself to or twine around an upright structure. This climbing habit may not develop until the plant is well-established.

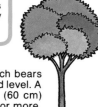

TREE

A tree is a perennial plant which bears only one woody stem at ground level. A mature tree may be only 2 ft (60 cm) high or as tall as 100 ft (30 m) or more, depending on variety.

CONIFER

A conifer is a perennial plant which bears cones. These cones are nearly always made up of scales, but there are exceptions (e.g Yew). The leaves are usually evergreen but there are exceptions (e.g Larch). A mature conifer may be only 1 ft (30 cm) high or as tall as 100 ft (30 m) or more, depending on variety. A popular group bought primarily for their architectural shape.

HEDGE

A formal hedge is a continuous line of shrubs, trees or conifers in which the individuality of each plant is lost. An informal hedge is a line of shrubs, trees or conifers in which some or all of the natural outline of the plant is preserved. It is usual to plant just one variety, but this is not essential. The traditional hedge is formal and may need to be clipped regularly in summer — see page 35. A flowering hedge is informal and is cut when the flowers fade.

The Basic Features of Easy-care Types

A number of popular shrubs and climbers are not classed as easy-care plants. Some must be pruned every year to ensure that they continue to flower freely or to prevent growth becoming straggly or over-rampant. There are others which are damaged by cold winds or heavy frosts. Some of these shrubs or climbers may be in your garden and will need the treatment set out in textbooks such as The Tree & Shrub Expert. When buying new plants, however, it is a good idea to choose from the easy-care lists (pages 32–35) whenever you can. These plants have all or nearly all of the basic features which make them simple to care for once they are established in your garden.

 HARDY The plant should be able to withstand the wet and cold of winter without the need for any form of protection. Avoid plants which have a 'not fully frost hardy' warning — examples include the Rock Rose (Cistus) and Hibiscus.

 NEAT COMPACT HABIT There are a number of shrubs and trees which must have their stems cut back each year to prevent them becoming leggy and unattractive. Examples include Buddleia, Sumach, Forsythia and Tamarisk. Always check the anticipated height before buying a tree for your garden — this is often a problem with Willows and many conifers. Some climbers (e.g Wisteria and Russian Vine) may be too vigorous for a small garden.

 TOUGH The plant should be able to stand up to cold winds, some degree of shade, a reasonably wide range of soil types and it should not be unduly sensitive to droughts. Plants which do not qualify include Japanese Maple, Winter Hazel, Fabiana, Eucryphia and Tree Poppy.

 PRUNING NOT ESSENTIAL The easy-care flowering plant is able to live its whole life or go on for many years without pruning. This does not apply to some old favourites like Lilac, Spanish Broom and Philadelphus which must be pruned every year to maintain their free-flowering habit.

 EVERGREEN There is a double benefit here. The plant remains clothed with foliage in winter so that some or all of its decorative effect is maintained in the barren months. In addition this retention of foliage means that there are no dead leaves which have to be brushed or raked up in late autumn. The term 'evergreen' can be misleading. The foliage may be red, bronze, purple, gold or edged with white or yellow. Green is just one of the colours.

 LONG-LIVING The plant should last for many years in your garden provided the soil is reasonably free-draining. There are a number of shrubs such as Broom (Cytisus) which occasionally die after a few years for no apparent reason.

Buy Good Quality Stock

Container-grown plants are now the most popular type of planting material — you can see what you are getting and transplanting can take place at any time of the year. You will still have to choose with care. Look for the danger signs — wilted leaves, dead or diseased stems, split containers, dry soil or a thick root growing through the base. Don't buy the biggest size you can afford — large and old specimens often take a long time to establish. View 'bargain offers' with caution — they are sometimes low quality stock which will never do well. A good type of bargain offer consists of rooted cuttings in pots, but you will have to wait some time before they reach flowering size.

Easy-care Trees, Shrubs & Climbers

NAME	TYPE	NOTES	HEIGHT AFTER 10 YEARS
AUCUBA (Aucuba)	S : E	Variegated varieties of A. japonica are popular — planted where little else will grow	7 ft (2.1 m)
BERBERIS (Barberry)	S : D or E	Popular and easy spiny shrub — many varieties are available. Yellow or orange flowers in spring	1–8 ft (30 cm–2.4 m)
BETULA (Birch)	T : D	Graceful specimen tree — a dwarf variety of B. pendula (Silver Birch) is the one to grow	12 ft (3.6 m)
CHAENOMELES (Japonica)	S : D	An old favourite — grown for its spring flowers (white, pink or red) and autumn fruits	5 ft (1.5 m)
CHOISYA (Mexican Orange)	S : E	Attractive rounded bush with glossy foliage. Flat heads of white flowers in spring	6 ft (1.8 m)
COTINUS (Smoke Bush)	S : D	Feathery flower-heads in midsummer — leaves turn golden in autumn. Sold as Rhus cotinus	10 ft (3 m)
COTONEASTER (Cotoneaster)	S : D or E	Lots of showy berries and good foliage colours in autumn. Varieties in all shapes and sizes	½–15 ft (15 cm–4.5 m)
CRATAEGUS (Hawthorn)	T : D	Specimen tree or hedging plant. White, pink or red flowers in late spring — red or orange berries in autumn	25 ft (7.6 m)
DAPHNE (Daphne)	S : D or E	The deciduous D. mezereum is the popular variety — purple-red flowers in February	3 ft (90 cm)
ELAEAGNUS (Oleaster)	S : D or E	The evergreen E. pungens 'Maculata' with yellow-splashed leaves is the popular variety	7 ft (2.1 m)
ERICA (Heather)	S : E	Many varieties from ground cover to framework shrubs. Most but not all need acid soil	½–10 ft (15 cm–3 m)
ESCALLONIA (Escallonia)	S : E	Choose one of the hybrids — e.g E. 'Apple Blossom'. Flowers are white, pink or red	6 ft (1.8 m)
EUONYMUS (Euonymus)	S : D or E	The popular ones are the variegated evergreens — e.g E. radicans 'Silver Queen'. Excellent ground covers	1–2 ft (30–60 cm)
GARRYA (Silk Tassel Bush)	S : E	Rounded bush with oval leaves — long and slender catkins drape down in January and February	10 ft (3 m)
GAULTHERIA (Checkerberry)	S : E	The best known one is G. procumbens — a shiny-leaved ground cover with white flowers	½ ft (15 cm)
GENISTA (Broom)	S : D	The one to grow is G. lydia — a spreading low bush with golden flowers in May–June	2 ft (60 cm)
HAMAMELIS (Witch Hazel)	S : D	Fragrant spidery flowers appear in winter before the leaves. Good autumn foliage colour	8 ft (2.4 m)
HEBE (Shrubby Veronica)	S : E	Many types available — some are tender. Choose a small variety such as H. 'Autumn Glory'	1½–3 ft (45–90 cm)
HEDERA (Ivy)	C : E	Widely used as a climber or ground cover. Many leaf variegations available — white, yellow or golden	10–15 ft (3–4.5 m)
HYDRANGEA (Hydrangea)	S or C : D	Many Lacecap and Mophead varieties are available — H. petiolaris is a self-clinging climber	5 ft (1.5 m)
HYPERICUM (St. John's Wort)	S : semi E	Yellow flowers all summer and autumn — a low-growing bush which will grow almost anywhere	2 ft (60 cm)

TYPE KEY

S : —	Shrub
T : —	Tree
C : —	Climber
— : D	Deciduous
— : E	Evergreen

Erica carnea 'Myretoun Ruby'

Euonymus japonicus 'Microphyllus Albus'

NAME	TYPE	NOTES	HEIGHT AFTER 10 YEARS
ILEX (Holly)	S : E	Many forms — smooth leaves, yellow berries etc. Buy a self-fertile one to ensure berry production	5-15 ft (1.5-4.5 m)
JASMINUM (Winter Jasmine)	S : D	The popular variety is J. nudiflorum — yellow flowers on lax leafless stems from November to February	10 ft (3 m)
LAVANDULA (Lavender)	S : E	Clumps of greyish-green leaves. White, pink or lavender flowers from July to September	1-2 ft (30-60 cm)
LONICERA (Honeysuckle)	S or C : D or E	A vast genus with a shrubby group and an even larger climbing group. Growth of climbers rather untidy	3-20 ft (90 cm-6 m)
MAHONIA (Mahonia)	S : E	Small ones widely used for growing under trees — large ones (e.g M. japonica) used as specimen plants	2-8 ft (60 cm-2.4 m)
OSMANTHUS (Osmanthus)	S : E	O. delavayi is the one to choose — white fragrant blooms on arching stems in April	5 ft (1.5 m)
PARTHENOCISSUS (Virginia Creeper)	C : D	Tall spreading vines used for wall cover. Leaves of P. tricuspidata turn bright red in autumn	30 ft (9.1 m)
PHORMIUM (Phormium)	T : E	P. cookianum 'Tricolor' with green/white/red leaves has an exotic palm-like appearance	4 ft (1.2 m)
PIERIS (Pieris)	S : E	An excellent choice for acid soil — young leaves are bright red and spring floral sprays are white	4 ft (1.2 m)
POTENTILLA (Shrubby Cinquefoil)	S : D	Choose one of the many varieties if you want an easy shrub which blooms from May to September	2-4 ft (60 cm-1.2 m)
PRUNUS (Prunus)	S : D or E	Evergreens include Portugal and Cherry Laurel — P. triloba (pink flowers) is a popular deciduous one	4-16 ft (1.2-4.8 m)
PRUNUS (Ornamental Cherry)	T : D	Very popular flowering tree — blooms between January and June depending on variety. Flowers single or double	3-25 ft (90 cm-7.6 m)
PYRACANTHA (Firethorn)	S : E	Widely planted wall shrub grown for its massed display of red or orange berries in autumn	6-12 ft (1.8-3.6 m)
RHODODENDRON (Azalea)	S : D or E	A low-growing evergreen or Japanese Azalea is a must for the mixed border if you have an acid soil	1-15 ft (30 cm-4.5 m)
RIBES (Flowering Currant)	S : D	R. sanguineum is seen everywhere. Pink or red flowers on pendent heads in spring. Quick growing	6 ft (1.8 m)
ROBINIA (Robinia)	T : D	R. pseudoacacia 'Frisia' is eye-catching — spreading layers of golden yellow leaves all season long	25 ft (7.6 m)
SALIX (Willow)	S or T : D	Ordinary varieties are far too large for most gardens — choose a dwarf like S. 'Kilmarnock'	5-10 ft (1.5-3 m)
SKIMMIA (Skimmia)	S : E	Neat and compact — white flowers in spring. Male and female plants needed for berry formation	3 ft (90 cm)
SORBUS (Mountain Ash)	T : D	Colourful graceful tree — white flowers, yellow or red berries and golden autumn leaves	15-25 ft (4.5-7.6 m)
SPIRAEA (Spiraea)	S : D	Spring-flowering varieties have white flowers — summer ones are deep pink or red	2-6 ft (60 cm-1.8 m)
VIBURNUM (Viburnum)	S : D or E	A vast genus of easy plants with winter- and spring-flowering as well as autumn-berrying types	5-10 ft (1.5-3 m)
VINCA (Periwinkle)	S : E	A trailing ground cover to carpet banks or bare ground with white or blue flowers all summer long	½ ft (15 cm)

Mahonia aquifolium

Potentilla 'Abbotswood'

Viburnum davidii

Easy-care Conifers

NAME	NOTES	SPECIES & VARIETIES			
		NAME	ULTIMATE HEIGHT	HEIGHT AFTER 10 YEARS	NOTES
ABIES (Fir)	Most firs are giants — choose with care	A. balsamea 'Hudsonia'	DWARF	1 ft (30 cm)	Good for rock gardens
		A. koreana	MEDIUM	6 ft (1.8 m)	Dark green foliage
CHAMAECYPARIS (False Cypress)	Very popular — scores of varieties are available, ranging from rockery dwarfs to stately giants	C. lawsoniana 'Allumii'	MEDIUM	6 ft (1.8 m)	Conical — blue-grey foliage
		C. l. 'Columnaris'	MEDIUM	8 ft (2.4 m)	Narrow, conical — good specimen tree
		C. l. 'Elwoodii'	DWARF	5 ft (1.5 m)	Popular — grey-green foliage
		C. l. 'Elwood's Gold'	DWARF	4 ft (1.2 m)	Branchlet tips golden-yellow
		C. l. 'Minima Aurea'	DWARF	1 ft (30 cm)	Compact pyramid — bright yellow
		C. l. 'Minima Glauca'	DWARF	1 ft (30 cm)	Round shrub — sea green foliage
		C. obtusa 'Nana Gracilis'	DWARF	2 ft (60 cm)	Dark green rounded sprays
		C. pisifera 'Boulevard'	DWARF	3 ft (90 cm)	Silvery-blue feathery sprays
JUNIPERUS (Juniper)	Popular ones are either dwarfs or spreading ground covers. All are easy to grow	J. chinensis	DWARF	5 ft (1.5 m)	Conical — blue-green foliage
		J. communis 'Compressa'	DWARF	1 ft (30 cm)	Columnar — grey-green foliage
		J. c. 'Depressa Aurea'	DWARF	1 ft (30 cm)	Spreading — golden foliage
		J. horizontalis 'Glauca'	PROSTRATE	1 ft (30 cm)	Spreading — blue carpet
		J. media 'Pfitzerana'	DWARF	4 ft (1.2 m)	Very popular — wide spreading
		J. squamata 'Meyeri'	DWARF	4 ft (1.2 m)	Erect — blue-grey foliage
		J. virginiana 'Skyrocket'	MEDIUM	6 ft (1.8 m)	Narrow column — blue-grey foliage
PINUS (Pine)	Pines are usually too tall — dwarf varieties are available	P. mugo 'Gnom'	DWARF	2 ft (60 cm)	Globular — rockery Pine
		P. nigra	TALL	10 ft (3 m)	Dark green foliage
		P. strobus 'Nana'	DWARF	2 ft (60 cm)	Spreading — silvery foliage
TAXUS (Yew)	Yews are generally slow-growing. Suitable for shade	T. baccata	MEDIUM	6 ft (1.8 m)	Dark green tree or hedge
		T. b. 'Fastigiata'	MEDIUM	6 ft (1.8 m)	Conical — Irish Yew
		T. b. 'Fastigiata Aurea'	MEDIUM	6 ft (1.8 m)	Yellow-edged dark green foliage
		T. b. 'Semperaurea'	DWARF	2 ft (60 cm)	Spreading — golden foliage
THUJA (Arbor-vitae)	Similar to Chamaecyparis. Good range of colours	T. occidentalis 'Rheingold'	DWARF	3 ft (90 cm)	Conical — bronzy foliage
		T. orientalis 'Aurea Nana'	DWARF	2 ft (60 cm)	Globular — golden foliage
		T. plicata	TALL	16 ft (4.8 m)	Pyramid — specimen tree
TSUGA (Hemlock)	Most types are too tall	T. canadensis 'Pendula'	DWARF	2 ft (60 cm)	Spreading — weeping branches

ULTIMATE HEIGHT KEY

PROSTRATE : under 1½ ft (45 cm)   **DWARF :** 1½–15 ft (45 cm–4.5 m)

MEDIUM : 15–50 ft (4.5–15.2 m)   **TALL :** over 50 ft (15.2 m)

Easy-care Hedging Plants

NAME	TYPE	NOTES
ACER (Maple)	F : D	The Field Maple (A. campestre) hedge is much less common than Beech, but it flourishes in all soil types and the plants quickly grow together. Trim in late autumn
BERBERIS (Barberry)	I : D or E	Several evergreens such as B. stenophylla, B. darwinii and B. julianae make splendid informal hedges with yellow flowers in spring. B. thunbergii is deciduous. Trim Berberis after flowering
BERBERIS (Barberry)	D : D	B. thunbergii atropurpurea 'Nana' produces a compact formal hedge about 1½ ft (45 cm) high. The foliage is reddish — trim after leaf fall
CARPINUS (Hornbeam)	F : D	A quick-growing hedge which quickly reaches 8 ft (2.4 m) if left untrimmed. Usually keeps its dead leaves like Beech. Reliable in heavy soil. Trim in late summer
ESCALLONIA (Escallonia)	I : E	The evergreen E. macrantha is popular in coastal areas as it tolerates salt-laden air. Red flowers appear in June — trim when the flowers fade
FAGUS (Beech)	F : D	F. sylvatica has green- and purple-leaved varieties — all can be trimmed to produce a tall formal hedge. Brown leaves persist over winter. Trim in August — tackle any hard pruning in February
ILEX (Holly)	F : E	I. aquifolium forms a dense barrier which is colourful when berries are present or a variegated variety has been used. Trim in late summer
LAVANDULA (Lavender)	D : E	A popular low-growing hedge — purple flowers, aromatic grey foliage. Cut off stalks once flowers fade — trim the plants to shape in April
PRUNUS (Laurel)	F : E	Portugal Laurel (P. lusitanica) and Cherry Laurel (P. laurocerasus) make fine tall hedges with dense shiny leaves, but plenty of room is required. Trim in March
PRUNUS (Sloe)	I : D	The Sloe or Blackthorn (P. spinosa) has long been used for hedging fields — white flowers appear in spring. Cut back unwanted growth in winter
PYRACANTHA (Firethorn)	I : E	The popular P. coccinea can be used for hedging but P. rogersiana is usually recommended. Cut back in summer to expose berries
RIBES (Flowering Currant)	I : D	This plant is usually grown as a shrub, but it can be grown at 1 ft (30 cm) intervals to produce an attractive hedge. Trim when the flowers fade
ROSA (Rose)	I : D	Some Shrub Roses make good hedges, but only informal ones as they cannot stand regular trimming. Remove unwanted growth in spring
TAXUS (Yew)	F : E	This old favourite need not be dull — there are bright golden varieties. No trouble, but it is slow to establish. Trim in late summer
THUJA (Thuja)	F : E	Western Red Cedar (T. plicata) is the conifer to grow if you want cypress-like foliage. Unlike the popular Leyland Cypress it needs only one trim (March) each year

TYPE KEY

F : — Formal Hedge — a line of hedging plants which are trimmed to form a smooth surface. Foliage types are generally treated this way

I : — Informal Hedge — a line of hedging plants which are not trimmed to form a smooth surface. Flowering types are generally treated this way

D : — Dwarf Hedge — a line of low-growing hedging plants which are pruned to 3 ft (90 cm) or less. The hedge may be formal or informal

— : D Deciduous

— : E Evergreen

A Word of Warning

Avoid many of the popular types such as Privet, Lawson's Cypress, Leyland Cypress, Box etc. These hedging plants are not easy-care varieties as they have to be trimmed at least 3 times during the summer months. An easy-care hedging plant is one which requires just one trim a year. A few other hedging plants, such as Honeysuckle, have been omitted from the list because they have an untidy growth habit.

PLANT PROPERLY

The Golden Rule

Poor planting is the usual cause of poor results. Make sure that the soil around each newly planted specimen will encourage root growth, and keep this area moist if the weather is dry. You must also make sure that there is enough space between the shrubs or trees.

Not all planting material sold by shops, garden centres and mail order companies is top quality and it is easy to blame the plant if a tree or shrub fails. Disappointment, however, is more likely to be due to mistakes at planting time at the start and then at pruning time in later years. There is more to planting than digging a hole and dropping in the plant. Read carefully the section on Planting in Chapter 2 — it may be that planting is a little more complex than you thought but following the rules will save you both time and money in the long run. For the first year it will be necessary to water thoroughly during dry spells in late spring or summer, although watering should not be necessary once the plant is established.

Planting each specimen carefully is important, but planting too closely is the commonest fault. It is easy to see why this happens. The plants from the garden centre are usually small, and when planted at the recommended distances the spaces in between look bare. But the plants *will* mature, and if you have planted them too closely there are only two alternatives. You can either dig out some of the cramped shrubs (which is the more sensible but less popular choice) or you can hack them back each year, which takes time and also destroys much of their beauty. The right thing to do is to follow the guide below.

Recommended Planting Distance for most shrubs and trees

Add the mature height of A and the mature height of B (check the label).

Divide the answer by 3 for the recommended planting distance

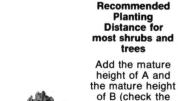

PLANTING DISTANCE

You will need to fill the bare space until the shrubs or trees are mature. There are several alternatives:

- Plant a number of 'filler' shrubs between the newly-planted choice shrubs or trees. These fillers should be popular types which can be bought cheaply as bargains — Ribes, Spiraea etc. Progressively remove them as the choice plants develop and need more room.

  or

- Use perennials and bulbs in the same way.

  or

- Fill the space with ground cover shrubs or perennials. Some of these may have to be removed as the choice specimens develop.

  or

- Put in bedding plants for an annual display.

  or

- Put down polyethylene sheeting and cover with mulching material (shredded bark, compost, gravel etc). This will keep out weeds and keep in moisture but it is of no decorative value.

PRUNE PROPERLY

Cutting back severely at the wrong time may lead to the loss of a whole season's flowers and occasionally to the death of the shrub. The standard advice is to check the precise pruning requirement of each individual plant before reaching for the secateurs or shears. In the easy-care garden a simpler approach is followed. Check the table below and follow the instructions for once-a-year pruning. With plants chosen from the easy-care lists it is not essential to prune if the tree or shrub has healthy branches and it is not crowding into other trees and shrubs.

Pruning for Growth

LIGHT PRUNING

HEADING BACK involves the removal of the ends of the branches. This pruning technique is called **TRIMMING** when all the tips are removed *en masse*. This stimulates the buds below the cuts to burst into growth.

The long-term effect is to produce a shrub which is smaller and denser than one left unpruned.

HARD PRUNING

THINNING involves the removal of entire branches back to the main stem. This diverts extra energy to the remaining branches.

The long-term effect is to produce a shrub which is larger and more open than one left unpruned.

When & How to Prune

The following table is a general guide to pruning. There are a number of exceptions and the rule to follow is that if you are in doubt — don't prune.

DECIDUOUS SHRUBS WHICH BLOOM BEFORE THE END OF MAY

Time: As soon as flowering is over — do not delay

Cut out all weak, dead and awkwardly-placed shoots and then remove overcrowded or invasive branches.

Flowers are produced on old wood. Some of the branches which have borne flowers should therefore be cut back — new, vigorous growth will develop and this will bear flowers next season.

DECIDUOUS SHRUBS WHICH BLOOM AFTER THE END OF MAY

Time: January–March — do not wait until growth starts

Cut out all weak, dead and awkwardly-placed shoots and then remove overcrowded or invasive branches.

Flowers are produced on new wood. If flowering has been poor cut back some of the old branches to stimulate fresh growth for next year's flowers.

FLOWERING CHERRIES & CONIFERS

Time: Late summer or autumn — never in winter

Cut out dead wood and overcrowded or invasive branches.

EVERGREEN SHRUBS

Time: May

Cut out all weak, dead and awkwardly-placed shoots and then remove overcrowded or invasive stems. With some of these plants (Santolina, Rhododendron, Buxus etc) hard pruning can be used to regenerate bushes with leggy stems.

HEDGES

Time: See page 35. Trim an informal flowering hedge when blooms have faded

The established formal hedge should be kept at 4–6 ft (1.2–1.8 m) and the top should be narrower than the base. You can use shears but an electric hedgetrimmer will save time. Place plastic sheeting at the base of the hedge — this will make clipping removal much easier.

CHAPTER 5

ROSES

There is no need here to sing the praises of roses — millions of words have been written over the years about their fascination and millions of people regard them as their favourite flower. What has to be said in this book is that most roses are work-intensive and do not belong in the easy-care garden. For most gardeners roses mean Hybrid Teas and Floribundas, and here you have to prune before growth starts and to dead-head when blooms fade. Feeding is necessary for top-quality blooms and worst of all is the need for regular spraying. A large number of varieties are susceptible to both mildew and black spot, and this means using a fungicide at regular intervals. Of course you need not bother, but with roses which have low disease resistance the usual result is a mass of black-spotted yellow leaves which can be an eyesore in late summer.

Despite the work involved in maintenance and the danger of disease most gardeners who are either too busy or unable to spend much time in the garden still feel that they must have some Hybrid Teas or Floribundas. This is a good thing, but there is no point in having disease-ridden plants if you are not going to spray. The answer is to choose varieties noted for their reliability and good disease resistance — see the list on pages 41 and 42.

The great attraction of modern Hybrid Teas and Floribundas is their repeat-flowering habit as well as the beauty of their blooms. Shrub Roses are much less popular and are usually thought of as plants which bloom only once in summer. Even if this was true it would still be no reason for treating them as Cinderella plants. The flowering period is often longer than for many other shrubs and with some types there is a colourful display of fruits in the autumn. But the single-flush reputation for *all* Shrub Roses is not true — many are repeat flowering. Another misconception is that all Shrub Roses are tall and wide-spreading — there are dwarfs as well as giants in the list on pages 41 and 42. This group of roses will thrive where Hybrid Teas may fail and both pruning and maintenance are very simple — Shrub Roses should be more widely used in the easy-care garden.

You may be looking for a rose which can be grown against a wall or up a trellis or pergola. Look for an easy-care Climber and not a Rambler — this latter group is prone to mildew and bears only a single flush during the season. In addition the old wood has to be cut back each year and so pruning is a tiresome chore.

CHOOSE EASY-CARE TYPES

The Golden Rule

Most roses call for an appreciable amount of work during the year — pruning, dead-heading, regular spraying etc. To save time and effort choose easy-care Shrub Roses which need little attention. When buying Modern Roses make sure that they have good disease resistance — see below.

The Basic Groups

HYBRID TEA

The most popular class — the flower stems are upright and the flowers are shapely. The typical Hybrid Tea bears blooms which are medium-sized or large, with petals forming a distinct central cone. The flowers are borne singly or with several side buds. The top choice for the flower vase, but the HT will not put up with neglect like many Shrubs and Floribundas.

FLORIBUNDA

Second only to the Hybrid Tea in popularity. The Floribunda bears its flowers in clusters or trusses, and several blooms open at one time in each truss. This class is unsurpassed for providing a colourful and long-lasting bedding display, but in general the flower form is inferior to that of the HT. Both petal size and number vary greatly from one variety to another.

PATIO

In the 1980s the low-growing varieties of Floribunda Roses were separated and given their own name — the Patio Roses. These neat 1½ ft (45 cm) high bushes have become popular and there are many fine types. They make excellent tub plants — hence the name, but they are also widely used for the front of the border. The continuity of bloom is generally very good.

MINIATURE

This class has increased in popularity due to its novelty and versatility. Both leaves and flowers are small, and under normal conditions the maximum height is less than 1½ ft (45 cm) — many varieties are considerably shorter. Miniature Roses can be used for edging, growing in tubs and in rockeries and for bringing indoors as temporary pot plants.

SHRUB

A large and highly varied class of roses with only one feature in common — they do not fit neatly into any other group. The typical Shrub is taller than the types used for bedding and is a Species variety (clearly related to a wild rose), an Old Garden Rose (dating back to pre-HT days) or a Modern Shrub Rose (mostly repeat flowering).

CLIMBER

A class of roses which if tied to a support can be made to climb. There are two groups. Ramblers have long pliable stems which need to be cut back each year and there is only one flush of flowers. Choose instead a stiff-stemmed Climber. The easy-care ones have a repeat flowering habit plus good disease resistance.

GROUND COVER

Shrub Roses with a distinctly spreading or trailing growth habit have been moved to a class of their own — the Ground Cover Roses. The leafy mounds are useful for covering banks or manhole covers, but nearly all varieties can grow to 2 ft (60 cm) or more when mature. There are a few which reach only 1½ ft (45 cm) or less.

Easy-care Roses

NAME	TYPE	COLOUR	NOTES	HEIGHT
ALEXANDER	HT	Orange vermilion	A tall bush with bright blooms which needs space — good for hedging	5 ft (1.5 m)
ANNA FORD	P	Deep orange	Small yellow-eyed flowers cover the glossy foliage of this small bush. Slightly fragrant	1½ ft (45 cm)
ANNE HARKNESS	F	Apricot yellow	The upright branches bear large trusses of double blooms in mid and late summer	4 ft (1.2 m)
BALLERINA	S	Pale pink	Tiny white-eyed flowers are borne in Hydrangea-like heads. Growth is bushy	3 ft (90 cm)
CANARY BIRD	S	Canary yellow	The rose to grow to herald in the flowering season — blooms in May	6 ft (1.8 m)
CECILE BRUNNER	S	Shell pink	A small bush with clusters of tiny double flowers. Repeat flowering	2½ ft (75 cm)
COMPASSION	C	Apricot pink	Free-flowering and fragrant — the double blooms are borne on stiff stems	10 ft (3 m)
DARLING FLAME	M	Orange vermilion	Most Miniatures are prone to mildew and black spot — this is a healthy one	1 ft (30 cm)
DORTMUND	C	Bright red	Single blooms with a white eye — can be kept pruned as a large shrub	10 ft (3 m)
DUBLIN BAY	C	Deep red	Both foliage and double flowers are attractive, but it is more bush- than climber-like	8 ft (2.4 m)
ELINA	HT	Ivory	The yellow-centred flowers are large and fragrant — growth is upright	3½ ft (1.1 m)
FELLOWSHIP	F	Deep orange	A neat bush with abundant foliage — the medium-sized double blooms are fragrant	2½ ft (75 cm)
FLOWER CARPET	GC	Rose pink	Spreads to 4 ft (1.2 m). Large clusters of double flowers — excellent disease resistance	2½ ft (75 cm)
FRAU DAGMAR HARTOPP	GC	Pale pink	Spreads to 4 ft (1.2 m). Large single blooms followed by large hips. Strongly scented	3 ft (90 cm)
FREEDOM	HT	Bright yellow	A reliable bush with glossy leaves and masses of medium-sized flowers	2½ ft (75 cm)
GROUSE	GC	Blush white	Spreads to 10 ft (3 m). There is just one flush of small single flowers	2 ft (60 cm)
HERTFORDSHIRE	GC	Carmine pink	A compact low-growing Ground Cover — spreads to 3 ft (90 cm). Flowers are single	1½ ft (45 cm)
KORRESIA	F	Bright yellow	An excellent Floribunda — the blooms are large, fragrant and double. Continuity is very good	2½ ft (75 cm)
LITTLE BO-PEEP	GC	Pale pink	Spreads to 1½ ft (45 cm). A Miniature Ground Cover with dense growth. Blooms semi-double	1 ft (30 cm)
MARJORIE FAIR	S	Carmine red	Large heads of tiny white-eyed flowers and masses of glossy leaves. Repeat flowering	4 ft (1.2 m)
PANDORA	M	Cream	This bushy Miniature has inherited the good disease resistance of its parent Darling Flame	1 ft (30 cm)

TYPE KEY

HT : Hybrid Tea (other name — Large Flowered Bush)
F : Floribunda (other name — Cluster-flowered Bush)
P : Patio (other name — Dwarf Cluster-flowered)
M : Miniature
S : Shrub
C : Climber
GC : Ground Cover

Rosa 'Flower Carpet'

Rosa 'Korresia'

NAME	TYPE	COLOUR	NOTES	HEIGHT
PENELOPE	S	Shell pink	The most popular Hybrid Musk — large clusters of semi-double blooms starting in June	4 ft (1.2 m)
PHYLLIS BIDE	C	Dull pink	Small double blooms are borne in wide trusses above the glossy foliage	8 ft (2.4 m)
PINK FAVOURITE	HT	Deep pink	The large high-centred flowers appear throughout the summer on sturdy stems	2½ ft (75 cm)
PRETTY POLLY	P	Rose pink	A rounded compact bush bearing many clusters of medium-sized blooms. Slightly fragrant	1½ ft (45 cm)
QUEEN ELIZABETH	F	Pale pink	An excellent rose which needs space — grow it as a specimen bush or as a hedge	6 ft (1.8 m)
RED TRAIL	GC	Bright red	Spreads to 5 ft (1.5 m). Trusses of yellow-eyed semi-double flowers are freely borne	3 ft (90 cm)
REGENSBERG	P	Pale pink	The white-eyed blooms are remarkably large for such a small bush. Fragrant	1½ ft (45 cm)
ROSA MOYESII GERANIUM	S	Scarlet	Bright red single flowers appear in May or June — the showy hips follow later	8 ft (2.4 m)
ROSA RUBRIFOLIA	S	Deep pink	Flowers are small and fleeting — the attractive features are the purplish leaves and red hips	6 ft (1.8 m)
ROSA RUGOSA ALBA	S	White	A typical Rugosa — wrinkled disease-free leaves, fragrant flowers and attractive hips	5 ft (1.5 m)
ROSA RUGOSA SCABROSA	S	Magenta pink	The single flowers are large and fragrant, appearing from spring to autumn	5 ft (1.5 m)
ROSE GAUJARD	HT	Rose red	The petals have a silvery reverse — a free-flowering rose which is easy to grow	3½ ft (1.1 m)
ROSERAIE DE L'HAY	S	Wine red	The double purplish blooms are fragrant. A reliable rose — excellent for hedging	7 ft (2.1 m)
SAVOY HOTEL	HT	Pale pink	A vigorous bushy rose — the blooms are large and double. Slightly fragrant	2½ ft (75 cm)
SILVER JUBILEE	HT	Rosy salmon	A popular bedding variety — the flowers are double and the healthy foliage is dense	2½ ft (75 cm)
SOUTHAMPTON	F	Apricot orange	The slightly ruffled flowers are flushed with red — good choice for a large bed	3½ ft (1.1 m)
SURREY	GC	Pink	Spreads to 4 ft (1.2 m). A free-flowering plant with double medium-sized blooms. Fragrant	2½ ft (75 cm)
SWEET DREAM	P	Apricot orange	Neat, cushion-like growth — the fragrant double blooms stand up well to rain	1½ ft (45 cm)
SWEET MAGIC	P	Orange	Large clusters of small flowers fade from deep orange to golden yellow. Pronounced fragrance	1½ ft (45 cm)
THE FAIRY	S	Pale pink	Tiny rosette-like blooms are borne in large trusses from late summer onwards	2½ ft (75 cm)
THE TIMES	F	Blood red	The eye-catching blooms open flat. Big trusses appear above the abundant foliage	2½ ft (75 cm)
YESTERDAY	S	Rose pink	Long flowering season — the flat blooms are semi-double. Trim for ground cover	3 ft (90 cm)

Rosa 'Pink Favourite'

Rosa rugosa 'Scabrosa'

Rosa 'Silver Jubilee'

PLANT PROPERLY

The Golden Rule

You will want your roses to last for 20 years or more with a minimum of attention. This calls for choosing easy-care varieties, but proper planting is also a vital step. Pay careful attention to the site, planting time, spacing and planting technique.

Pick the Right Spot

PLENTY OF SUN is required to produce top quality roses, but light shade during the afternoon is beneficial.
ROSES CANNOT STAND DEEP AND CONTINUOUS SHADE

SUITABLE SOIL is necessary, and fortunately this can be achieved in nearly all gardens. Ideally it should be a medium loam, slightly acid and reasonably rich in plant foods and humus. A high clay content is not desirable (add organic matter) and a high lime content is harmful. Soil in which roses have grown for more than 5 years is liable to be 'rose sick' which means that new roses will not thrive after planting. Where possible choose a spot in which roses have not grown before, but this is not always possible. To reduce the chance of rose sickness when planting in a rose bed add a bark-based compost to the soil before planting and apply a hoof and horn fertilizer.
ROSES CANNOT THRIVE IF THE SOIL IS POOR

PLENTY OF AIR is required to produce healthy plants. Bush and standard roses do not like being shut in by walls and overhanging plants.
ROSES CANNOT STAND BEING PLANTED UNDER TREES

SHELTER FROM COLD WINDS is helpful. A nearby hedge or fence is useful, but it should not be close enough to shade the bush. Avoid planting in the lowest part of the garden if it is a 'frost pocket'.
ROSES DO NOT THRIVE IN EXPOSED SITES

REASONABLY FREE DRAINAGE is essential, so break up the subsoil if necessary.
ROSES CANNOT STAND BEING WATERLOGGED

Pick the Right Time

BARE-ROOT PLANTS

APR	MAY	JUNE	JULY	AUG	SEPT	OCT	NOV	DEC	JAN	FEB	MAR

Soil condition is as important as the calendar. The ground must be neither frozen nor waterlogged. Squeeze a handful of soil — it should be wet enough to form a ball and yet dry enough to shatter when dropped on to a hard surface

BEST TIME
in nearly all gardens, as the soil is warm enough to produce some root growth before winter

BEST TIME
in very heavy soils and in cold exposed areas with high rainfall

CONTAINER-GROWN PLANTS

APR	MAY	JUNE	JULY	AUG	SEPT	OCT	NOV	DEC	JAN	FEB	MAR

BEST TIME

BEST TIME

These roses can be planted at any time of the year, but some times are better than others. The soil must be in the right condition (see above), and autumn or spring planting allows some root development before the summer drought

Space at the Right Distance

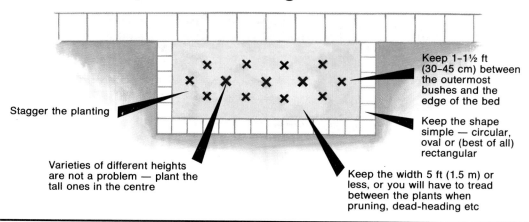

Stagger the planting

Varieties of different heights are not a problem — plant the tall ones in the centre

Keep 1–1½ ft (30–45 cm) between the outermost bushes and the edge of the bed

Keep the shape simple — circular, oval or (best of all) rectangular

Keep the width 5 ft (1.5 m) or less, or you will have to tread between the plants when pruning, dead-heading etc

ROSE TYPE	DISTANCE BETWEEN SIMILAR PLANTS
MINIATURE ROSES	1 ft (30 cm)
PATIO ROSES	1½ ft (45 cm)
HYBRID TEA & FLORIBUNDA BUSHES Compact varieties	1½ ft (45 cm)
HYBRID TEA & FLORIBUNDA BUSHES Average varieties	2 ft (60 cm)
HYBRID TEA & FLORIBUNDA BUSHES Tall varieties	2½ ft (75 cm)
LOW-GROWING SHRUBS	3 ft (90 cm)
GROUND COVER ROSES	expected spread: average 3½ ft (1.1 m)
STANDARDS	4 ft (1.2 m)
SHRUBS	half of expected height: average 5 ft (1.5 m)
WEEPING STANDARDS	6 ft (1.8 m)
CLIMBERS	7 ft (2.1 m)

Plant in the Right Way

Just digging a hole and popping in the plant will not do. If you have not been successful with roses in the past then study the rules in Chapter 2 before you start to plant either bare-root or container-grown bushes. Note that standards are treated in the same way as any other tree and note that climbing roses should be kept away from the base of the house wall as described for other woody climbers. Whenever possible planting should take place immediately the roses arrive. If a delay is unavoidable then the package of bare-root plants can be left unopened for about a week — make sure that they are kept in a frost-proof place. If the delay is likely to be more than a week the roses should be heeled in. Dig a shallow V-shaped trench and spread the plants as a single row against one side of it. Cover the roots and lower part of the stems with soil and tread down. Label with some form of permanent tag if there are several varieties — paper labels attached by the supplier may fade or rot away.

PRUNE PROPERLY

How to Prune

❀ MINIATURE ROSES • SHRUB ROSES • CLIMBERS

Cutback Method ✗

Don't cut these roses back like Hybrid Teas or Floribundas — very little pruning is required.

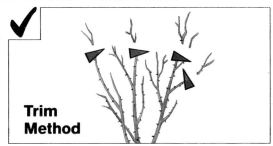

Trim Method ✓

Cut off dead and sickly growth and then merely trim to shape if necessary to avoid overcrowding.

❀ PATIO ROSES • HYBRID TEAS • FLORIBUNDAS

Traditional Method ✗

The first step is to remove all dead, diseased and damaged wood, and then cut out weak and soft growth. Congested stems in the centre of the bush are removed and finally the remaining healthy stems are dealt with. Each shoot is cut back, using a sloping cut close to an outward-facing bud. The amount removed is ⅓–⅔ of the shoot, depending on the rose type.

Rough Method ✓

Nothing could be simpler — the bush is cut to half its height with secateurs or a hedge trimmer. Leave all the weak and twiggy growth. Cut out dead wood to the base if you want to. Surprisingly, bushes pruned by this method produce more and bigger blooms than roses cut back by the laborious Traditional Method recommended in the textbooks.

When to Prune

Early spring pruning is recommended for autumn- and winter-planted roses and for established plants. If the bushes or standards are to be planted in the spring, prune just before planting. The best time to prune is when growth is just beginning. The uppermost buds will have begun to swell but no leaves will have appeared.

Dead-heading

The regular removal of dead blooms from Hybrid Teas, Floribundas and Patio Roses improves the appearance of the bush and stops energy being diverted to fruit production. The standard way is to cut the flower stem with secateurs to where there is a strong bud, but it is easier and better to snap off the dead flower by hand.

CHAPTER 6

HARDY PERENNIALS

Hardy perennials are the non-woody and non-bulbous plants which come up year after year. Most are herbaceous, which means that the leaves die in winter, but a few keep their foliage and so provide a little greenery during the dormant season.

The traditional home for these plants is the herbaceous border — the feature which more than anything else symbolises The British Garden. For the first half of the 20th Century no self-respecting sizeable garden was complete without one, and all sorts of rules were laid down by Gertrude Jekyll and others for their creation. The border has to be backed by a wall or hedge and it has to be at least 9 ft (2.7 m) wide. The hardy perennials which fill it are set out in large informal blocks and contrasting flower forms are put next to each other. Colour clashes have to be avoided and neighbouring plants are chosen to bloom in sequence.

The expertly-planned and well-kept herbaceous border is a splendid sight during the summer months, but it is a thing to admire and not to make. This type of border requires a lot of attention — many of the plants have to be staked and dead-headed during the growing season and then divided and replanted every few years. There is another drawback even if you don't object to the work involved — for part of the year even the best of herbaceous borders has a bare and unattractive look.

The place for hardy perennials is in a mixed bed or border — this feature owes as much to the idea of the old cottage garden as to the principles of the herbaceous and shrub border. The basic concept is to have colour and interest all year round. You can choose from the whole range of garden plants with one vital proviso — the subjects chosen must be suitable for the location in question. Roses with evergreen and flowering shrubs provide a woody and colourful framework — within this setting the hardy perennials are planted in groups of three or five. Some bold architectural types such as Acanthus and Cortaderia can be planted singly as focal points, but with nearly all others there is a distinctly spotty effect if you grow single isolated specimens. Put in bedding plants and bulbs to fill the bare spots close to the front of the border.

Choose your hardy perennials with care. Avoid the short-lived ones (e.g Anchusa, Aquilegia and Perennial Flax) and those like Geum that need lifting and dividing every couple of years. For the back of the border pick tall bushy plants such as Aruncus rather than weaker-stemmed types such as Helenium.

CHOOSE EASY-CARE TYPES

Easy-care Hardy Perennials

NAME	SITE & SOIL	NOTES
ACANTHUS (Bear's Breeches)	Sun or light shade — well-drained soil	A. spinosus is the usual one — height 4 ft (1.2 m), spacing 2½ ft (75 cm). Flowers (white/purple) in July–September
ACHILLEA (Yarrow)	Sunny site — well-drained soil	Yellow flat-topped flower-heads in June–September. Look for a dwarf 2 ft (60 cm) variety — e.g 'Moonshine'
AJUGA (Bugle)	Sun or light shade — ordinary soil	Creeping ground cover — height 4 in. (10 cm), spacing 1½ ft (45 cm). Choose a coloured leaf variety
ALCHEMILLA (Lady's Mantle)	Sun or light shade — well-drained soil	A. mollis is an old favourite — height 1½ ft (45 cm), spacing 1½ ft (45 cm). Flowers (small, greenish-yellow) in June–August
ANEMONE (Anemone)	Sun or light shade — well-drained soil	Saucer-shaped blooms in August–October — leaves are deeply lobed. Height 3 ft (90 cm), spacing 1½ ft (45 cm)
ARTEMISIA (Wormwood)	Sun or light shade — well-drained soil	A. ludoviciana is grown for its silver feathery foliage — height 3 ft (90 cm), spacing 2 ft (60 cm)
ARUNCUS (Goat's Beard)	Light shade — ordinary soil	Dark green foliage and branching plumes of white flowers in June. Height 5 ft (1.5 m), spacing 4 ft (1.2 m)
ASTILBE (Astilbe)	Light shade — moist soil	Feathery plumes of tiny flowers in June–August — many varieties are available. Height 2½ ft (75 cm), spacing 1½ ft (45 cm)
ASTRANTIA (Masterwort)	Light shade — well-drained soil	A. major produces pink-tinged white flower-heads in June–September. Height 2 ft (60 cm), spacing 1½ ft (45 cm)
BERGENIA (Bergenia)	Sun or light shade — well-drained soil	Ground cover with large, fleshy leaves. Hyacinth-like flower spikes in March–April. Height 1½ ft (45 cm), spacing 1½ ft (45 cm)
COREOPSIS (Tickseed)	Sunny site — well-drained soil	C. grandiflora is the usual one — yellow Daisy-like flowers in June–September. Height 1½ ft (45 cm), spacing 1½ ft (45 cm)
CORTADERIA (Pampas Grass)	Sun or light shade — well-drained soil	Grow C. selloana as a focal point — 1½ ft (45 cm) silvery plumes on 4-10 ft (1.2-3 m) stalks in October
CRAMBE (Crambe)	Sun or light shade — well-drained soil	A bold bushy plant with large leaves and sprays of tiny white flowers in June. Height 6 ft (1.8 m)
DICENTRA (Bleeding Heart)	Light shade — well-drained soil	D. spectabilis is the popular one — arching stems with white/pink flowers in May. Height 2½ ft (75 cm), spacing 1½ ft (45 cm)
DORONICUM (Leopard's Bane)	Sun or light shade — well-drained soil	D. orientale is an early-flowering dwarf — yellow Daisy-like flowers in April–May. Height 1 ft (30 cm), spacing 1 ft (30 cm)
EPIMEDIUM (Bishop's Hat)	Partial shade — ordinary soil	Ground cover for shade — turns bronze in autumn. April flowers are insignificant. Height 9 in. (22.5 cm), spacing 1 ft (30 cm)
ERIGERON (Fleabane)	Sun or light shade — well-drained soil	Looks like a small Michaelmas Daisy — flowers in June–August. Height 1½ ft (45 cm), spacing 1 ft (30 cm)
ERYNGIUM (Sea Holly)	Sunny site — well-drained soil	Thimble-shaped blue flowers above Thistle-like leaves in July–September. Height 2 ft (60 cm), spacing 1½ ft (45 cm)
EUPHORBIA (Spurge)	Sun or light shade — well-drained soil	Masses of flower-heads in May — colour is usually yellow but there is an orange one. Height 2 ft (60 cm), spacing 1½ ft (45 cm)
GERANIUM (Crane's-bill)	Sun or light shade — well-drained soil	Excellent ground cover — flowers (white, pink, red or blue) in May–August. Height 1½ ft (45 cm), spacing 1½ ft (45 cm)
HELLEBORUS (Hellebore)	Partial shade — moist soil	Two types — Christmas Rose (January–March) and Lenten Rose (February–April). Height 1 ft (30 cm), spacing 1½ ft (45 cm)
HEMEROCALLIS (Day Lily)	Sun or light shade — ordinary soil	Large Lily-like trumpets (pale yellow to deep red) in June–August. Height 3 ft (90 cm), spacing 2 ft (60 cm)

NAME	SITE & SOIL	NOTES
HEUCHERA (Coral Flower)	Sun or light shade — well-drained soil	Tiny bell-shaped blooms (white, pink or red) on top of slender stems in June–August. Height 2 ft (60 cm), spacing 1½ ft (45 cm)
HOSTA (Plaintain Lily)	Partial shade — ordinary soil	Excellent ground cover grown for its attractive foliage and spikes of flowers in July–August. Height 2 ft (60 cm), spacing 2 ft (60 cm)
IRIS (Iris)	Sunny site — well-drained soil	Some of the Bearded Irises (hairs on petals) are easy-care plants. Example is I. pallida — height 2½ ft (75 cm), spacing 2 ft (60 cm)
LIRIOPE (Lily-turf)	Sunny site — well-drained soil	L. muscari has spikes of violet flowers in September–November. Height 9 in. (22.5 cm), spacing 1 ft (30 cm)
NEPETA (Catmint)	Sunny site — ordinary soil	Popular edging plant — small lavender flowers in May–September and aromatic leaves. Height 2 ft (60 cm), spacing 1½ ft (45 cm)
OENOTHERA (Evening Primrose)	Sunny site — well-drained soil	Grow a hardy one like O. 'Fireworks' — yellow Poppy-like flowers in June–August. Height 1½ ft (45 cm), spacing 1½ ft (45 cm)
POLYGONUM (Knotweed)	Sun or light shade — ordinary soil	Evergreen ground cover. Choose a P. affine variety — height 1 ft (30 cm), spacing 2 ft (60 cm), pink flowers June–October
PRIMULA (Primula)	Partial shade — humus-rich soil	Many are easy-care plants. An example is P. denticulata — flowers in March–April, height 1 ft (30 cm), spacing 1 ft (30 cm)
PULMONARIA (Lungwort)	Partial shade — moist soil	Leaves are generally silver-spotted and evergreen. Height 1 ft (30 cm), spacing 1 ft (30 cm), flowers in March–May
RUDBECKIA (Coneflower)	Sun or light shade — ordinary soil	Dark-centred blooms in July–September. Popular one is R. fulgida 'Goldstrum' — height 2 ft (60 cm), spacing 2 ft (60 cm)
SALVIA (Salvia)	Sun or light shade — well-drained soil	Blue flowers in July–September. Usual species is S. superba — height 3 ft (90 cm), spacing 1½ ft (45 cm)
SAXIFRAGA (Saxifrage)	Sun or light shade — humus-rich soil	The most popular one is London Pride with starry flowers in May–July — height 1 ft (30 cm), spacing 1½ ft (45 cm)
SEDUM (Stonecrop)	Sunny site — well-drained soil	S. spectabile is an old favourite with 4 in. (10 cm) wide flower-heads in August–October — height 1½ ft (45 cm), spacing 1 ft (30 cm)
SOLIDAGO (Golden Rod)	Sunny site — well-drained soil	Grow a dwarf such as S. 'Golden Thumb' — yellow flower-heads in August–September. Height 1½ ft (45 cm), spacing 1½ ft (45 cm)
STACHYS (Lamb's Ears)	Sun or light shade — well-drained soil	S. lanata is a good ground cover — woolly leaves and mauve flowers in July–August. Height 1½ ft (45 cm), spacing 1½ ft (45 cm)
TIARELLA (Foam Flower)	Sun or light shade — ordinary soil	Good ground cover with evergreen leaves and tiny white flowers in May–July — height 1 ft (30 cm), spacing 1 ft (30 cm)
TOLMIEA (Piggyback Plant)	Sun or light shade — ordinary soil	A house plant which can be used as ground cover — tiny flowers in June. Height 9 in. (22.5 cm), spacing 1½ ft (45 cm)
TRADESCANTIA (Spiderwort)	Sun or light shade — ordinary soil	Hardy varieties have sword-like leaves and silky flowers in June–September. Height 1½ ft (45 cm), spacing 1½ ft (45 cm)
VERONICA (Speedwell)	Sun or light shade — well-drained soil	Wide range of heights. V. spicata has spikes of small flowers in June–July — height 1½ ft (45 cm), spacing 1 ft (30 cm)

Doronicum plantagineum

Geranium pratense

Hemerocallis 'Stafford'

CHAPTER 7

BEDDING PLANTS

The sales of bedding plants have more than doubled in the past 10 years and it is easy to see why. In spring the garden centres are filled with packs and pots of plants in full flower, and most gardeners find the promise of instant gardening irresistible. In the morning there is an empty bed — after a visit to the garden centre, High St shop or market stall the bare ground is transformed into a brightly coloured plot by the evening. The basic small garden approach has been to set out Tulips and other bulbs in autumn and then to plant around them with lines of Wallflowers, Forget-me-nots and other spring-flowering bedding plants. Out they come in late spring and in go the summer-flowering hardy and half-hardy plants — Alyssum, Lobelia, Geraniums and the rest.

The rapid rise in the popularity of containers has added another dimension, and now more bedding plants are set out in pots, tubs, hanging baskets etc than in beds and borders. So there are more uses than there were, and there are also more varieties. Each year we are offered exciting new introductions and the 1990s have seen the appearance of Lotus, Bidens, Scaevola, Diascia and Bacopa in garden centres.

There are other advantages to bedding plants in addition to the instant gardening effect. You do not have to live with your mistakes as the planting only lasts a season, and the cost is not usually high. Another virtue is that many bedding plants stay in bloom all season long.

Instant gardening, but not easy-care gardening. The basic problem is that the plants must be dug out each year and new ones bedded out in either autumn or late spring. In addition many need regular dead-heading and as their root system is shallow all will need regular watering during dry spells.

These are serious drawbacks and some writers on low-maintenance gardening say that there is no place for bedding plants. This, perhaps, is going too far. The large bed or border filled with regimented rows in park-like fashion is definitely out, but there are areas in the easy-care garden where bedding plants could and should be used. Be guided by the Choose Easy-care Types and Plant Properly sections in this chapter.

Where money as well as time is short then consider sowing hardy annual seeds where they are to grow as well as or instead of buying bedding plants. Calendulas will fill bare spaces with colour and Sweet Peas and Nasturtiums will clothe arches and fences in summer.

CHOOSE EASY-CARE TYPES

Easy-care Bedding Plants

NAME	TYPE	NOTES	HEIGHT
AGERATUM (Floss Flower)	HHA	Masses of powder-puff flowers (mid June–end October) on bushy plants. For edging choose a compact variety	6–18 in. (15–45 cm)
ALYSSUM (Sweet Alyssum)	HA	Popular edging plant — tiny, honey-scented flowers (mid June–end September) cover the small-leaved cushions	3–6 in. (7.5–15 cm)
ANCHUSA (Bugloss)	HA	Anchusa is usually grown as a perennial but you can buy the annual A. capensis (blue, mid June–end September)	18 in. (45 cm)
BEGONIA (Bedding Begonia)	HHA	Free-flowering plant useful in semi-shade. Flowers (mid June–mid October) are white, pink or red — buy in flower	4–12 in. (10–30 cm)
BELLIS (Daisy)	HB	Single or double Daisies (April–June) for edging or containers. Giants have 2 in. (5 cm) wide blooms	3–6 in. (7.5–15 cm)
BRASSICA (Ornamental Cabbage)	HA	The flat heads of Ornamental Cabbage and Kale have colourful and decorative leaves — October–January display	9–18 in. (22.5–45 cm)
CALENDULA (Pot Marigold)	HA	An old cottage-garden favourite — yellow or orange flowers in mid May–mid September. Use dwarfs for edging	9–24 in. (22.5–60 cm)
CHEIRANTHUS (Wallflower)	HB	Wide range of colours (off white–deep red) for mid March–mid June flowers. Grow Siberian Wallflower for late blooms	9–24 in. (22.5–60 cm)
CHLOROPHYTUM (Spider Plant)	HHP	This foliage house plant makes an attractive centrepiece for summer display in a container. Prefers partial shade	12–18 in. (30–45 cm)
CINERARIA (Dusty Miller)	HHA	C. maritima is widely grown for its ferny silvery-grey leaves. The small yellow flowers are not showy	6–15 in. (15–37.5 cm)
COREOPSIS (Tickseed)	HA	The annual forms of Coreopsis bear Marigold-like flowers (early July–end September). Yellow, red or brown	12 in. (30 cm)
DIANTHUS (Annual Carnation)	HHA	There are a number of dwarf Annual Carnations which do not need staking. Fragrant flowers in June–October	9–18 in. (22.5–45 cm)
DIANTHUS (Sweet William)	HB	Flattened heads of densely-packed, Pink-like flowers in mid May–late July. Bicolours are popular	6–24 in. (15–60 cm)
DIASCIA (Diascia)	HP	A 1990s introduction — spurred open-faced flowers (early June–end September) on lax stems	12 in. (30 cm)

TYPE KEY

HA : Hardy Annual
HHA : Half-hardy Annual
HB : Hardy Biennial
HP : Hardy Perennial
HHP : Half-hardy Perennial

Begonia 'Starlet'

Cheiranthus cheiri 'Orange Bedder'

NAME	TYPE	NOTES	HEIGHT
ESCHSCHOLZIA (California Poppy)	HA	Very easy — sprinkle seed over bare ground in autumn or spring for June–September silky-petalled flowers	6–12 in. (15–30 cm)
FUCHSIA (Fuchsia)	HP or HHP	Many bushy varieties are available — trailers are useful for hanging baskets. Most have bell-shaped flowers	12–24 in. (30–60 cm)
GAZANIA (Gazania)	HHA	The most eye-catching S. African Daisy — flowers (end June–mid October) have a dark-rimmed yellow centre	9–15 in. (22.5–37.5 cm)
HELICHRYSUM (Helichrysum)	HHP	H. petiolatum is grown for its attractive display of felted leaves. Usual colour is silvery-grey	Length 24 in. (60 cm)
IBERIS (Candytuft)	HA	Domed clusters of fragrant flowers cover the foliage in mid May–mid September. White, pink, red or mauve	6–15 in. (15–37.5 cm)
IMPATIENS (Busy Lizzie)	HHA	One of the most popular bedding plants, flowering continually in sun or partial shade in early June–mid October	6–18 in. (15–45 cm)
KOCHIA (Burning Bush)	HHA	Looks like a young conifer — the neat bushy growth is made up of feathery foliage. Autumn colour	18–36 in. (45–90 cm)
LIMNANTHES (Poached Egg Plant)	HA	An attractive plant which may be hard to find. White-edged yellow flowers in early June–mid October	4 in. (10 cm)
LOBELIA (Lobelia)	HHA	The No.1 edging and trailing plant for containers. Blue is the usual colour — white and red available	4–6 in. (10–15 cm)
MALCOLMIA (Virginia Stock)	HA	Not really a bedding plant. Not transplanted — just a sprinkle of seed and then flowers 1–2 months later	4 in. (10 cm)
NEMOPHILA (Nemophila)	HA	Low-growing carpeting plant — blue flowers in mid June–early October. Best sown where it is to flower	6–12 in. (15–30 cm)
NICOTIANA (Tobacco Plant)	HHA	Grow one of the modern dwarfs rather than an old-fashioned tall one. Flowers mid June–mid October	12–24 in. (30–60 cm)
NIGELLA (Love-in-a-mist)	HA	Very easy — just sow seed in autumn or spring where it is to grow. Flowers mid June–end August	12–24 in. (30–60 cm)
PELARGONIUM (Geranium)	HHP	Bedding Geraniums are the most important of the bold bedding plants — flowers mid June–end October	6–18 in. (15–45 cm)
PETUNIA (Petunia)	HHA	Showy, funnel-shaped blooms in mid June–mid October. Multifloras are free-flowering — P. 'Surfinia' is a trailer	6–18 in. (15–45 cm)
PRIMULA (Primrose)	HP	The most popular type for spring bedding is Polyanthus (P. variabilis). Yellow-eyed flowers in March–May	9–12 in. (22.5–30 cm)
SCAEVOLA (Scaevola)	HHP	Lax stems. Flowers (mid June–end September) are distinctive — there are petals on one side only	Length 12 in. (30 cm)
TAGETES (Afro-French Marigold)	HHA	Good choice — flowers (mid June–end October) larger than French ones, plants smaller than African Marigolds	12–18 in. (30–45 cm)
TAGETES (Tagetes)	HHA	These are the dwarf half-hardy Marigolds. Popular as edging plants — flowers mid June–mid October	6–9 in. (15–22.5 cm)
TROPAEOLUM (Nasturtium)	HA	Grow for edging, ground cover or climbing — flowers mid June–end October. Sow seeds rather than transplanting	6–18 in. (15–45 cm)
VERBENA (Verbena)	HHA	Small Primrose-like flowers (mid June–mid October) crown the stems. Upright and trailing types available	6–18 in. (15–45 cm)
VIOLA (Viola, Pansy)	HA or HB	They will grow in partial shade and stay in flower for 4–6 months. Winter-flowering Universal strain is now popular	6–9 in. (15–22.5 cm)

Helichrysum petiolatum 'Moonlight'

Impatiens 'Tango'

Limnanthes douglasii

BUY PROPERLY

The Golden Rule

Success involves more than just choosing the right varieties. It means going to the right supplier at the right time of the year and buying plants in the right condition and in the right container to suit your needs and pocket.

The Right Supplier

As an easy-care gardener you will buy plants rather than raise your own from seed, and as a general rule you will get what you pay for. The best source of supply for bedding plants ready for setting out is the garden centre — the range is usually large and varied, and advice is generally available. You will find plants on offer in greengrocers, florists, department stores etc — poor growing conditions can sometimes be a problem here, but convenience is often a great advantage. Market stalls usually offer the lowest-priced plants, but most experts warn against them — half-hardy plants are often put out before the danger of frost has passed and you will find only the old favourites here. Still, there are many good market stalls with knowledgeable owners. Finally there are the mail order companies. Bedding plants are rarely purchased from this source, but the mail order seed companies have come into their own recently as a source of plugs for growing on in compost until they reach the planting out stage.

The Right Time

Spring-flowering hardy annuals can be bought and planted out in April or early May when the weather and soil are suitable. Half-hardy annuals and perennials should be bought later as they must not be set out until the danger of frost has gone — this means waiting until mid or late May in southern counties and as late as early June in exposed northern areas. Spring-flowering plants such as Daisies and Wallflowers should be bought and planted in October.

The Right Condition

Buy plants which are compact and sturdy, and are growing in compost which is moist. There should be no wilted leaves nor drooping stems. Pot plants are generally sold in flower. With strips and trays it is wise to buy plants in bud with just a few open blooms, but some (e.g Impatiens, Begonia and Marigolds) are nearly always sold in flower. Do not buy Geraniums or Petunias in flower unless they are in pots or packs.

The Right Container

TRAY

The tray is the traditional method of buying bedding plants. It is the cheapest way to buy for immediate planting, but roots are damaged when they are torn apart at planting time. Plastic trays have replaced wooden ones. Never buy a few plants wrapped in newspaper.

STRIP

The strip has become the most popular way to buy bedding plants. The plants are grown in a series of snap-off strips which are made of rigid white polystyrene or flimsy plastic. Each strip contains from 3 large plants (e.g Geraniums) to 10–12 small annuals (e.g Antirrhinums).

PACK

The pack is made of flimsy plastic and consists of 4–24 individual pots. Each pot contains a single plant and is usually detached at the time of sale. More expensive per plant than strips, but there is no root disturbance at planting time. Packs are becoming increasingly popular.

POT

The individual rigid pot is the most expensive way to buy bedding plants, but this is the container for top-quality stock. Pots are usually plastic but clay ones are still used. Peat pots can be planted directly into the soil. Pots are the way to buy a few choice plants.

PLUG

A plug is larger and more advanced than a seedling — it is a small but well-rooted plant raised in a cellular tray by the grower. Economical — they are bought in units of 35. Use for planting directly into a hanging basket or into a small pot of compost for growing on before planting out.

PLANT PROPERLY

The Golden Rule

Setting out bedding plants is so much easier than planting trees, shrubs and roses, but this does not mean that there are no rules. Both arrangement and spacing are important, and so is good drainage. Finally, the planting operation itself calls for various ways to ensure that the transplants get off to the best possible start.

Arrangement

The creation of a formal bed calls for planting in geometric shapes. This entails marking out the pattern before you begin and after planting doing those tasks to ensure a uniform display. This means regular dead-heading and replacing poor specimens with plants kept in reserve. A lot of work for an out-of-fashion style.

It is better to use bedding plants as part rather than the whole of a bed or border planting scheme. Use them in informal clumps between other plants. Here differences between neighbouring plants are not a problem, nor is the loss of an occasional specimen. The other major use is in containers — see pages 56–59 for details.

Spacing

Ideally you should look at a book such as The Bedding Plant Expert to find the recommended spacing between plants, but you can use the following general guide. For low-growing and average-sized plants use the expected height as the spacing distance — see pages 52–53. For tall plants space at ⅔ of the anticipated height.

Planting

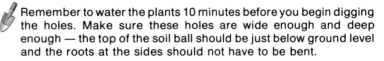 Follow the general planting rules listed in Chapter 2. Some particular points to watch out for are set out below.

 Remember to water the plants 10 minutes before you begin digging the holes. Make sure these holes are wide enough and deep enough — the top of the soil ball should be just below ground level and the roots at the sides should not have to be bent.

Tease the roots apart (don't cut them) when removing plants from a tray or strip. To extract a plant from a flimsy pot squeeze the bottom so that the soil ball pops out. Handle plants by the soil or leaves, never by the stems.

Gently water in after planting using a watering can without a rose.

CONTAINERS

The Basics

PLANT

Bedding plants are the favourite types but many plants ranging from tall trees to tiny alpines can be grown. The planting may be for a permanent display or for a seasonal one which is removed when the flowers have faded

WATERING SPACE

A gap must be left between the top of the container and the surface of the compost or mulch. This space is filled with water at watering time

CONTAINER

The world of containers is dominated by the well-known types such as pots, tubs, window boxes and hanging baskets, but almost any receptacle will do if it has a number of basic properties. It must be waterproof, although clay/terracotta loses water from the surface and hanging baskets need a liner. It must be stable and it must resist rot, rust and corrosion when exposed to the weather — it should also be frost-proof if required for permanent planting. It must be non-toxic to plants and it must hold enough compost to support the plants you intend to grow. Finally, water must drain away quickly

MULCH

An optional extra which is widely used with alpines. A shallow surface layer of crushed stone or gravel reduces water loss and inhibits weed growth

GROWING MEDIUM

Traditionally a soil or peat-based compost is used, but types based on coir etc are now available. The medium must be free-draining and contain a supply of fertilizer

DRAINAGE LAYER

In large containers crocking and a layer of gravel are needed

DRAINAGE HOLES

Usually but not always present in shop-bought containers. Adequate drainage is vital. Plastic pots often contain numerous small holes. Large terracotta and wooden containers should have at least one hole ½ in. (1 cm) or more across every 6 in. (15 cm)

LEGS

Bricks, small blocks or shop-bought terracotta legs should be used to raise the container above the ground or paving. This allows free drainage, prevents soil pest entry and reduces the risk of rot in wooden containers

BASE

A firm base is necessary. Exceptions — window boxes, hanging baskets and wall-mounted units

DRIP TRAY

The commonest type is the plastic or terracotta saucer. It acts as a water reservoir, but do not keep it constantly filled with water

or

GROUND or PAVING

Nearly all free-standing containers are stood either on bare earth or a paved area such as a patio. This base must be both firm and level

or

MOVABLE TROLLEY

This is the best type of base if the container is heavy and you intend to move it from one part of the garden to another during the season or indoors in winter

The Advantages

PLANTS ARE EASIER TO REACH

This is an important consideration for physically challenged people. Using tall containers can remove the need to stoop for such jobs as planting and dead-heading.

PLANTS NOT SUITED TO YOUR SOIL CAN BE GROWN

The soil type of your garden may be unsuitable for the plants you wish to grow, and a lot of work could be involved in changing it to ensure success. With container growing all you have to do is choose a suitable compost. By using a lime-free mixture you can have Azaleas and Camellias in a chalky garden, and you can grow Alpines to perfection on a clayey site.

LESS CHANCE OF PEST DAMAGE

Plants get a high degree of protection against slugs and some soil pests.

PLANTS CAN BE MOVED ONCE THE DISPLAY IS OVER

A potted rose bush in full bloom obviously deserves a prime spot such as the patio, but once the flowering season is over you can move the container to a less prominent site.

GROUND IS NOT NEEDED

For the millions without a garden, containers provide a way to have a bedding plant display on balconies, windows and walls. For those with a garden there are still many places for tubs, pots etc on paved areas, patios, pathways, porches and walls. Plants can be grown right next to the house.

PLANT DISPLAY IS IMPROVED

Small bedding plants are brought closer to eye level and weak-stemmed ones can be allowed to droop and trail. Tender types can be given the protection of a sunny wall. Bold flowers, trees and shrubs can be given an extra dimension as focal points.

BARE OR DULL AREAS CAN BE IMPROVED

The outstanding reason for having planted-up containers in the garden is to add a splash of living colour or shape to an otherwise dull area. Doors and windows can be framed, large expanses of bare wall can be enlivened, and the monotony of paved backyards, courtyards and patios can be removed. Another virtue is the introduction of a third dimension to a two-dimensional one.

EYESORES CAN BE HIDDEN

Manhole covers can be masked with a collection of movable tubs or pots.

TENDER PLANTS CAN BE GROWN OUTDOORS

Tubs and pots containing tender perennials such as Palms and Orange trees can be brought into a conservatory or greenhouse in autumn. The containers are put out again in the spring when the danger of frost has passed. Small containers can be kept in an unheated room if you do not have a greenhouse.

PLANTS CAN BE TAKEN WITH YOU WHEN YOU MOVE

Containers and the plants they hold can be taken with you without the need for digging up and transplanting.

The Problems

Growing bedding plants and other types in containers is not an 'easy' way to garden. First of all, there are more decisions to make than with open-ground gardening. You must choose the right container, and that is not easy with the vast assortment on offer with prices ranging from the very cheap to the ridiculously expensive. Then you must choose a suitable growing medium, the best situation for the container and finally the plants which will flourish in the chosen environment. In addition there is a need for extra care for the growing plants. The amount of soil or compost available is limited so the watering and feeding requirements are greater than in the open garden. In addition permanent plants in a poorly-insulated pot can suffer in a severe winter.

WATER SHORTAGE

Attractive displays can be created in wide and shallow pots but the compost will dry out quickly and so daily watering will be necessary in hot and dry weather. Another problem container is the small pot or basket. The amount of compost present will not hold much water — enough for only a day or two of active plant growth.

Always buy the largest container you can afford and which is suitable for the site you have chosen. To avoid very frequent watering the pot or tub should be at least 9 in. (22.5 cm) wide and deep. A leafy shrub or tree will need a container which is at least 1½ ft (45 cm) wide and 1 ft (30 cm) deep.

By far the most popular types of hanging basket are made of wire or plastic. Both hold a relatively small amount of compost and are free-draining, so that daily watering may be necessary in dry weather. Buy a wire basket with a diameter of 14 in. (35 cm). To make watering easier consider an up-down mechanism such as a spring-loaded holder if the basket is over head high.

The self-watering basket is a boon for the gardener who cannot water every day in hot and dry weather. Several models are available — the basic principle is a water reservoir at the base together with capillary matting below the compost. The matting is kept constantly wet by the reservoir so that you only need to water every 1–2 weeks.

There is nothing basically wrong with scattering containers around the garden — baskets on the wall, tubs by the entrance, pots on the patio etc but the effect can be 'bitty' if all the containers and plants are different. In addition moving around with a watering can or hosepipe may be laborious.

Grouping a number of containers together heightens the impact. A large centre of interest can be created by using containers of different heights with a mixture of a few bold specimens and a groundwork of smaller types. Equally important is the fact that all the pots can be watered at the same time.

FOOD SHORTAGE

The nutrients in the compost will only last for 6–8 weeks, after which you will have to feed every 2–4 weeks if you use a standard liquid fertilizer. It is much better to push one or more slow-release fertilizer spikes or blocks into the compost — this will provide nutrients for the whole season.

FROST DAMAGE

Badly insulated pots (plastic, terracotta, fibreglass, thin wood, metal or earthenware) pose a real danger if they contain plants in winter. The compost may freeze solid leading to root death — the answer is to tie bubble plastic or sacking around the pot if it holds a valuable over-wintering plant.

The Plants

Most people fill their containers exclusively with bedding plants or a mixture of bedding plants and bulbs. As a general rule it is a good idea to pick more compact varieties than are used in outdoor bedding and to set them more closely together than you would do in a garden bed.

The tallest plants are placed in the centre or along the back depending on the viewing direction. You can use any of the plants listed on pages 52–53, but if you have just a few containers there is no need to restrict yourself to these easy-care ones. You can use plants needing support such as Love-lies-bleeding, and uncommon types such as Lantana, Lotus, Cleome, Canna etc which are more demanding than the common-or-garden bedding plants.

A large container can look uncomfortably bare from November to March. One solution is winter bedding with Universal Pansies, Winter Heather and Primula 'Crescendo'. Alternatively you can fill part of the container with permanent evergreens (Skimmia, Ivy, Dwarf Conifers etc) for year-round display and rely on bedding plants between them for a spring to autumn splash of colour.

CHAPTER 8

BULBS

Bulbs are excellent easy-care plants — they are so much easier to handle than tiny seeds or bulky container plants, and their large built-in food supply gives them a good start in life. However, there are two provisos — you must choose the right ones and you must plant them in the right place.

First of all, the right ones. The easy-care bulbs are hardy with a good reputation for reliability, and can be left in the ground to come up year after year. Many popular bulbs have to be lifted and stored each year — Garden Tulips, Hyacinths and nearly all Gladioli are dug up when the foliage has shrivelled and so are not considered to be easy-care plants. Botanical (Species) Tulips and Gladioli byzantinus are left in the ground and so are Narcissi, Crocuses, Snowdrops and Grape Hyacinths, but you shouldn't restrict yourself to the spring-flowering favourites. On pages 62–63 you will find a number of summer- and autumn-flowering ones which are well worth trying.

The second proviso is that you must plant bulbs in the right place. When considering where to plant them you should remember two important points. The main one is that bulb foliage dies down once flowering is over and this can be quite unsightly with large plants. Unfortunately it cannot be cut off until it is brown and withered and so you must think of ways of hiding these yellowing leaves. A good technique is to grow bulbs through ground-hugging plants such as Ajuga and Thyme — another way is to plant a group of bulbs close to hardy perennials which produce their leaves as the foliage of the bulbs starts to fade. Another point to remember when deciding where to plant is the fact that many bulbs spread quite rapidly by self-seeding or offsets, so don't set them too close to choice and delicate plants which may be overrun.

One of the attractive ways to use bulbs is to naturalise them in rough lawn or woodland. The classic technique is to drop handfuls of bulbs on to the ground and plant them where they fall. Do not cut the grass until the bulb leaves are brown and withered.

So far we have considered the basic requirements for easy-care bulbs — they must be the right ones and must be planted in the right place. But the basic rules of bulb growing must also be followed. Good drainage is essential if the bulbs are to flourish for years, and the planting hole should be the right depth. As a general rule large bulbs such as Narcissi should be covered to twice their own height with soil or compost and most small bulbs are covered to about their own height. Dig the hole a little deeper than this recommended depth and put a thin layer of peat or grit at the base before putting in the bulb.

CHOOSE EASY-CARE TYPES

The Golden Rule

You should choose hardy types which can stay in the ground over winter. Do not plant at less than the recommended depth and make sure that there is not an air pocket between the bottom of the bulb and the top of the soil in the hole.

Easy-care Bulbs

NAME	SITE & SOIL	NOTES
ALLIUM (Flowering Onion)	Sunny site — well-drained soil	In early or midsummer clusters of flowers appear on leafless stalks — these blooms may be wide- or narrow-petalled. Height 9 in. (22.5 cm), planting depth 4–6 in. (10–15 cm)
ANEMONE (Windflower)	Sun or light shade — well-drained soil	The Daisy-flowered Anemones are the easy ones. The first to flower is A. blanda (February–April) — A. apennina is a little later. Height 6 in. (15 cm), planting depth 2 in. (5 cm)
BRIMEURA (Spanish Hyacinth)	Sun or light shade — well-drained soil	Flower stalks bear 10–15 blue or white bells in early summer — uncommon but worth trying. Height 6 in. (15 cm), planting depth 4 in. (10 cm)
BULBOCODIUM (Spring Saffron)	Sunny site — well-drained soil	The young flowers are goblet-shaped and look like a Crocus, but they open wide as they mature. Height 4 in. (10 cm), planting depth 3 in. (7.5 cm), lavender flowers February–March
CAMASSIA (Quamash)	Sun or light shade — moist soil	A tall plant with stiff floral spikes of starry blooms in mid May–mid July. Height 24–36 in. (60–90 cm), planting depth 4 in. (10 cm). White, lavender or blue
CHIONODOXA (Glory of the Snow)	Sun or light shade — well-drained soil	Loose and dainty sprays bear about 10 blooms on each stalk. Usually white-centred blue — good for naturalising. Height 6–10 in. (15–25 cm), planting depth 3 in. (7.5 cm)
COLCHICUM (Autumn Crocus)	Sun or light shade — humus-rich soil	Wineglass-shaped flowers appear in late August–mid November before the leaves. Plant in midsummer. Height 6–9 in. (15–22.5 cm), planting depth 3 in. (7.5 cm)
CONVALLARIA (Lily of the Valley)	Partial shade — humus-rich soil	Dainty fragrant bells hang from arching stems. Can spread rapidly — good ground cover under trees. Height 8–12 in. (20–30 cm), planting depth 1 in. (2.5 cm)
CROCUS (Crocus)	Sun or light shade — well-drained soil	The spring-flowering species are very popular — goblet-shaped flowers in a wide range of colours. Autumn ones are available. Height 3–5 in. (7.5–12.5 cm), planting depth 3 in. (7.5 cm)
CYCLAMEN (Cyclamen)	Partial shade — humus-rich soil	Hardy types have 1 in. (2.5 cm) flowers — there are winter-, spring-, summer- and autumn-flowering varieties. Good ground cover. Height 4–6 in. (10–15 cm), planting depth 1 in. (2.5 cm)
ERANTHIS (Winter Aconite)	Sun or light shade — well-drained soil	A glossy yellow carpet of flowers appears in mid January–mid March. Each bloom has a frilly green collar. Height 3–5 in. (7.5–12.5 cm), planting depth 2 in. (5 cm)
ERYTHRONIUM (Dog's-tooth Violet)	Partial shade — humus-rich soil	E. dens-canis bears flowers in April–May with bent-back petals on top of wiry stems. Leaves have brown blotches. Height 6 in. (15 cm), planting depth 3 in. (7.5 cm)
FRITILLARIA (Fritillary)	Light shade — well-drained soil	F. meleagris is excellent for the rockery or naturalising in grass. Pendulous blooms (April–May) with a checkerboard pattern. Height 12 in. (30 cm), planting depth 5 in. (12.5 cm)
GALANTHUS (Snowdrop)	Light shade — moist soil	The herald of spring — white hanging bells appear in mid January–mid March. Dry bulbs transplant badly — divide in late spring. Height 6 in. (15 cm), planting depth 4 in. (10 cm)
GLADIOLUS (Gladiolus)	Sunny site — well-drained soil	You must pick one from the hardy Species group — G. byzantinus bears small red flowers in May and June. Height 24 in. (60 cm), planting depth 4 in. (10 cm)

PLANTING DEPTH
The distance between the top of the bulb and the soil or compost surface

NAME	SITE & SOIL	NOTES
IPHEION (Spring Starflower)	Sun or light shade — well-drained soil	Varieties of I. uniflorum bear 1 in. (2.5 cm) wide star-shaped blue or white flowers in April. Good for rockery or woodland. Height 6 in. (15 cm), planting depth 2 in. (5 cm)
IRIS (Iris)	Sunny site — well-drained soil	There are several types of Bulb Iris. The popular February–March ones are I. danfordiae (yellow) and I. reticulata (blue). Height 6 in. (15 cm), planting depth 3 in. (7.5 cm)
LEUCOJUM (Snowflake)	Sun or light shade — humus-rich soil	There are spring-, summer- and autumn-flowering ones — looks like a tall Snowdrop but petals are different. Height 6–24 in. (15–60 cm), planting depth 3 in. (7.5 cm)
LILIUM (Lily)	Sun or light shade — well-drained soil	Pick one of the Mid-Century Hybrids which is compact and sturdy such as L. 'Enchantment' — height 36 in. (90 cm), planting depth 6 in. (15 cm), flowers June–July
MUSCARI (Grape Hyacinth)	Sunny site — well-drained soil	Tiny bell- or flask-shaped flowers are massed on top of a leafless fleshy stem in mid March–mid May. Height 4–12 in. (10–30 cm), planting depth 3 in. (7.5 cm)
NARCISSUS (Narcissus, Daffodil)	Sun or light shade — well-drained soil	The single white and yellow varieties are seen everywhere — for something different choose doubles, pinks or split-coronas. Height 3–24 in. (7.5–60 cm), planting depth — twice bulb height
ORNITHOGALUM (Star of Bethlehem)	Sun or light shade — well-drained soil	O. umbellatum produces white starry flowers which face upwards and close at night. Grow in rockery or grassland. Height 12 in. (30 cm), planting depth 2 in. (5 cm)
OXALIS (Wood Sorrel)	Sunny site — well-drained soil	Take care. Make sure you choose a hardy non-invasive species such as O. adenophylla — height 3 in. (7.5 cm), planting depth 3 in. (7.5 cm), white/pink flowers June–July
PUSCHKINIA (Striped Squill)	Sun or light shade — well-drained soil	Easy and attractive, but less popular than its Bluebell relatives. Pale blue open bells with a dark stripe in March–April. Height 6 in. (15 cm), planting depth 2 in. (5 cm)
SCHIZOSTYLIS (Kaffir Lily)	Sun or light shade — humus-rich soil	Gladiolus-like spikes and Crocus-like pink or red flowers in mid September–early November. Height 24 in. (60 cm), planting depth 2 in. (5 cm)
SCILLA (Bluebell, Squill)	Sun or light shade — well-drained soil	Spikes of hanging blue bells in spring are not the only type — there are white and pink ones and varieties with round heads. Height 3–18 in. (7.5–45 cm), planting depth 2–4 in. (5–10 cm)
SISYRINCHIUM (Sisyrinchium)	Sunny site — humus-rich soil	S. striatum has whorls of creamy flowers on upright stems in May–June. Usually bought as a growing plant. Height 18 in. (45 cm), planting depth 1 in. (2.5 cm)
TULIPA (Tulip)	Sunny site — well-drained soil	Choose one of the Botanical (Species) Tulips such as T. kaufmanniana, T. fosteriana or T. greigii. Height 4–20 in. (10–50 cm), planting depth 4 in. (10 cm), flowers March-May

Eranthis hyemalis

Puschkinia scilloides

Tulipa greigii 'Plaisir'

CHAPTER 9
ROCK GARDEN PLANTS

Rock garden plants have a special charm. A number of widely differing types can be grown in a comparatively small space as most of them are both compact and low-growing. With care they can be used to produce an attractive and easy-care feature in the garden, but as outlined below there are pitfalls to avoid.

Before you begin you have two points to consider — the plants themselves and the home you plan to provide for them. With regard to the plants there is no simple definition which separates 'rock garden plants' from all the other sorts which are grown in the garden. There is no problem in defining the alpine group — these are species which were originally collected from mountainous regions such as the Alps and Himalayas. However, there are others such as the ones which originally came from the sea-shore (e.g Armeria) and many more from ordinary inland low-level habitats.

Some books say that rock garden plants are those varieties which look at home among the stones in the rockery, but a better definition is that they are the plants you can expect to find in the Rock Garden section in the catalogue and garden centre. Here you will find a large range of perennials together with dwarf conifers, dwarf shrubs and dwarf bulbs.

When making your choice there are two groups to watch out for. Firstly there are the easy but invasive ones such as Aubretia, Arabis, Alyssum saxatile, Cerastium and Saponaria — these rampant species can quickly overrun more delicate types. Secondly there are the non-invasive but difficult ones which cannot tolerate cold, soggy soil in winter and so need protection. On pages 66–67 there is a list of easy-care types, but there are many others — additional conifers like Pinus mugo 'Gnom', shrubs such as dwarf Azaleas and bulbs like Eranthis and Muscari.

You must also choose the right site. The rock garden or rockery (these terms are interchangeable) is the traditional home, but it is not the best choice for the easy-care gardener. It takes a good deal of effort and money to create and can be quite time-consuming to maintain in good condition. On pages 68–69 you will find ways of growing rock garden plants which involve less space and work. Whichever home you choose for your plants you must remember their basic needs — really good drainage, soil or compost to which grit has been added and a regular routine of weeding and trimming as necessary.

CHOOSE EASY-CARE TYPES

The Golden Rule

Choose with care — some rock garden plants are invasive and need cutting back regularly and there are others which are not able to survive a wet winter without protection. For most situations it is a good idea to have a range of sizes and shapes — use shrubs and conifers as well as alpines.

Easy-care Rock Garden Plants

NAME	SITE & SOIL	NOTES
ACAENA (New Zealand Burr)	Sun or light shade — ordinary soil	**HP** Spreading carpeter for cracks in paving. A. 'Blue Haze' forms silvery sheets — height 2 in. (5 cm), spread 24 in. (60 cm)
ACHILLEA (Alpine Yarrow)	Sunny site — sandy soil	**HP** Choose A. tomentosa — height 6 in. (15 cm), spread 12 in. (30 cm), heads of tiny yellow flowers in June–September
AETHIONEMA (Aethionema)	Sunny site — non-acid soil	**HP** Popular one is A. 'Warley Rose' with May–August rounded pink flower clusters. Height 6 in. (15 cm), spread 12 in. (30 cm)
ALLIUM (Flowering Onion)	Sunny site — ordinary soil	**B** Choose a non-invasive one — e.g A. beesianum. Height 12 in. (30 cm), planting depth 4 in. (10 cm), blue flowers in August
ANDROSACE (Rock Jasmine)	Sun or light shade — gritty soil	**HP** A. carnea is an evergreen cushion-forming type — height 4 in. (10 cm), spread 4 in. (10 cm), tiny pink flowers in April–May
ANEMONE (Windflower)	Sun or light shade — humus-rich soil	**B** A. blanda and A. apennina are described on page 62. Another rockery one is A. nemorosa — 8 in. (20 cm) high flowers in spring
ANTENNARIA (Cat's Ear)	Sunny site — ordinary soil	**HP** Good for cracks in paving — can be walked on. Height 4 in. (10 cm), spread 18 in. (45 cm), small flower-heads in May–June
AQUILEGIA (Alpine Columbine)	Sun or light shade — moist soil	**HP** Grow a dwarf species such as A. flabellata — white/violet flowers in June–July. Height 6 in. (15 cm), spread 6 in. (15 cm)
ARABIS (Rock Cress)	Sun or light shade — ordinary soil	**HP** A. Ferdinand-coburgii 'Variegata' is not invasive — height 4 in. (10 cm), spread 12 in. (30 cm), white flowers in spring
ARMERIA (Thrift)	Sunny site — ordinary soil	**HP** Hummocks of grass-like leaves — globular flower-heads in May–July. Height 8 in. (20 cm), spread 12 in. (30 cm)
ARTEMISIA (Artemisia)	Sunny site — ordinary soil	**HP** Grown for its leaves. A. schmidtiana 'Nana' forms mounds of silvery ferny foliage. Height 6 in. (15 cm), spread 12 in. (30 cm)
ASPERULA (Alpine Woodruff)	Sunny site — sandy soil	**HP** Choose a smooth-leaved one such as A. gussonii — height 4 in. (10 cm), spread 12 in. (30 cm), pink flowers in May–June
ASTER (Mountain Aster)	Sunny site — ordinary soil	**HP** A. alpinus has large white, blue or pink Daisy-like flowers in May–July. Height 6 in. (15 cm), spread 18 in. (45 cm)
ASTILBE (Rockery Astilbe)	Light shade — moist soil	**HP** The popular one is A. chinensis pumila — height 9 in. (22.5 cm), spread 12 in. (30 cm), mauve flowers in July–October
CAMPANULA (Bellflower)	Sunny site — non-acid soil	**HP** C. carpatica is popular — height 9 in. (22.5 cm), spread 12 in. (30 cm). Cup-shaped flowers (white or blue) in June–September
CHAMAECYPARIS (False Cypress)	Sunny site — acid soil	**DC** Choose one of the dwarf varieties of C. obtusa, such as 'Nana' (round, dark green) or C. pisifera 'Boulevard' (silvery-blue)
COTONEASTER (Cotoneaster)	Sun or light shade — ordinary soil	**DS** There are several ground-hugging Cotoneasters which are useful for clothing rocks or bare patches. Red berries in autumn
CROCUS (Crocus)	Sun or light shade — ordinary soil	**B** All can be grown in the rockery — see page 62. Favourite ones are the winter-flowering (February) varieties e.g C. 'Cloth of Gold'
CYCLAMEN (Cyclamen)	Partial shade — humus-rich soil	**B** All the hardy ones can be grown in the rockery — see page 62. C. hederifolium (flowers September–November) is the easiest
CYTISUS (Broom)	Sunny site — sandy soil	**DS** Pea-like flowers in May. Choose a true dwarf such as C. decumbens (6 in./15 cm) or C. ardoinii (8 in./20 cm)
DIANTHUS (Rockery Pink)	Sunny site — ordinary soil	**HP** Grey or green foliage. Examples are D. alpinus — 4 in. (10 cm) high and D. deltoides — 8 in. (20 cm). Flowers May–August
DICENTRA (Bleeding Heart)	Partial shade — ordinary soil	**HP** Arching stems, pendent flowers. Grow a dwarf — D. cucullaria has yellow-tipped white flowers in April–May, height 6 in. (15 cm)

NAME	SITE & SOIL	NOTES
DRABA (Whitlow Grass)	Sunny site — ordinary soil	**HP** Mounds of tiny leaves. The easiest is D. aizoides — height 3 in. (7.5 cm), spread 6 in. (15 cm), yellow flowers in April
DRYAS (Mountain Avens)	Sunny site — ordinary soil	**HP** Excellent ground cover. Popular one is D. octopetala — height 4 in. (10 cm), spread 24 in. (60 cm), white flowers in May–June
ERICA (Heather)	Sunny site — ordinary soil	**DS** For January–April flowers grow one of the varieties of E. carnea — height 9 in. (22.5 cm), spread 24 in. (60 cm)
ERIGERON (Fleabane)	Sunny site — ordinary soil	**HP** Choose a non-invasive species such as E. aureus — height 6 in. (15 cm), spread 24 in. (60 cm), golden flowers in July
ERINUS (Summer Starwort)	Sun or light shade — sandy soil	**HP** Small starry flowers. There is one species — E. alpinus. Height 3 in. (7.5 cm), spread 4 in. (10 cm), flowers April–August
ERODIUM (Storksbill)	Sunny site — ordinary soil	**HP** E. chrysanthum forms 9 in. x 9 in. (22.5 cm x 22.5 cm) mounds of ferny leaves. Cup-shaped yellow flowers appear in May–July
FRANKENIA (Sea Heath)	Sunny site — sandy soil	**DS** Prostrate plant with tiny leaves — looks like Heather. Height 3 in. (7.5 cm), spread 12 in. (30 cm). Flowers in July
GERANIUM (Crane's-bill)	Sunny site — ordinary soil	**HP** Flowers in May–August. Choose a rockery one such as G. cinereum — height 6 in. (15 cm), spread 12 in. (30 cm)
HEBE (Veronica)	Sun or light shade — ordinary soil	**DS** Choose a dwarf. H. pinguifolia 'Pagei' is an example — grey-green 9 in. (22.5 cm) mounds with white flowers in May–August
HYPERICUM (St. John's Wort)	Sunny site — ordinary soil	**DS** The most popular dwarf is H. olympicum — height 6 in. (15 cm), spread 12 in. (30 cm), yellow flowers in July–August
IRIS (Rockery Iris)	Sunny site — well-drained soil	**B/HP** See page 63 for Bulb Iris details. Non-bulb dwarfs include I. pumila — 4 in. (10 cm) and I. lacustris — 3 in. (7.5 cm)
JUNIPERUS (Juniper)	Sunny site — acid soil	**DC** Ground covers are available. J. sabina 'Tamariscifolia' is an example — height 12 in. (30 cm), spread 96 in. (240 cm)
NARCISSUS (Dwarf Narcissus)	Sun or light shade — ordinary soil	**B** Species and dwarf hybrids are available for February–March flowers. A typical example is N. 'Jack Snipe' — 8 in. (20 cm)
PHLOX (Dwarf Phlox)	Sunny site — moist soil	**HP** Many varieties available — height 4–6 in. (10–15 cm), spread 18 in. (45 cm), flowers in May–June
PRIMULA (Rockery Primrose)	Sunny site — ordinary soil	**HP** Large choice of varieties. P. wanda is popular — height 3 in. (7.5 cm), spread 6 in. (15 cm), flowers in March–May
SAXIFRAGA (Saxifrage)	Light shade — moist soil	**HP** Usual form is a low-growing group of rosettes or mossy sheets. Spring or early summer flowers are starry or saucer-shaped
SEDUM (Stonecrop)	Sunny site — ordinary soil	**HP** Many varieties — usual form (e.g S. spathulifolium) has low-growing stems, fleshy leaves and star-like flowers in June–July
SEMPERVIVUM (Houseleek)	Sunny site — ordinary soil	**HP** Ball-like rosettes of green or coloured fleshy leaves. Thick flower stems appear in July. A good choice for dry spots
THYMUS (Thyme)	Sunny site — sandy soil	**HP** T. serpyllum is the basic species — height 2 in. (5 cm), spread 24 in. (60 cm), flowers in June–July
TULIPA (Tulip)	Sunny site — ordinary soil	**B** Grow dwarf Species Tulips rather than Garden Hybrids. Examples are T. greigii, T. kaufmanniana and T. 'Fusilier'
VERONICA (Rockery Speedwell)	Sunny site — ordinary soil	**HP** V. prostrata is the most popular one — height 4 in. (10 cm), spread 18 in. (45 cm), flowers in May–August
VIOLA (Violet)	Sun or light shade — ordinary soil	**HP** Numerous types for March–August flowers are available — height 2–9 in. (5–22.5 cm), spread 6 in. (15 cm)

SITE & SOIL KEY
The prime requirement of rock garden plants is good drainage. Other basic requirements for top-quality plants are listed here.

NOTES KEY
HP : Hardy Perennial
B : Bulb
DS : Dwarf Shrub
DC : Dwarf Conifer

Anemone blanda

Iris pumila

CHOOSE THE RIGHT HOME

The Golden Rule

Rock garden plants can be used for edging beds, but the choice ones look better when grown in an area devoted solely to them. The rock garden is the traditional and perhaps the most attractive home, but it is a lot of work to make and maintain. Choose instead one of the alternatives.

A well-constructed **ROCK GARDEN** is perhaps the ideal home, but it is laborious to make and needs regular attention. To qualify as a 'rock garden' rather than a bed with a few stones it needs to be at least 8 ft x 4 ft (2.4 m x 1.2 m) and the rocks should be partly buried to make the rockery look like a sloping outcrop. If you want to build one despite the effort involved, study a book with detailed instructions and visit several good examples before you begin. You will need strong and able-bodied assistance and a planting mixture to fill the spaces between the stones. A standard mixture is 1 part topsoil, 1 part peat or well-rotted leafmould and 1 part grit or stone chippings. If you already have a rock garden then consider digging out the more invasive plants and replacing them with slower-growing types.

The **PAVING CRACKS** between the stones or slabs of paths or patios is a suitable home for many rock garden plants. They relieve the monotony of plain slabs, but only a few such as Antennaria and Thymus can withstand regular brushing and foot traffic. Dig out soil between the slabs using an old kitchen knife and gently insert and shake down the roots of a small plant or rooted cutting. Fill the hole with a planting mixture of 1 part topsoil, 1 part fine peat and 1 part coarse sand. Do this in autumn — alternatively you can add planting mixture to the dug-out hole and sow seeds in spring. Recommended plants include Acaena, Antennaria, Armeria, Dianthus, Erica, Saxifraga, Sedum and Thymus. If the base is free-draining you can make a more spectacular display by removing one or more slabs and then digging out enough foundation material for an 8 in. (20 cm) layer of planting mixture. Plant up and treat like a raised bed.

A **RAISED BED** is an increasingly popular home for rock garden plants. A height of 1½–3 ft (45–90 cm) is recommended and the retaining walls can be made with bricks, stone, reconstituted stone blocks or railway sleepers. Where space permits an upper terrace or a series of terraces can be built on the bed to create extra interest. Clear away perennial weeds before you begin and lay a concrete foundation if the walls are to be more than 1–1½ ft (30–45 cm) high. Provide weep-holes at the base if mortar-bonded bricks, blocks or stones are the building material. Fill with planting mixture (see Rock Garden above) — leave a 2 in. (5 cm) space at the top. Plant up after a few weeks. Choice and planting technique are the same as for the rock garden — trailers at the edge are especially important. Cover the surface with a 1 in. (2.5 cm) layer of stone chippings — use of a few larger stones on the surface is a matter of taste.

A **TROUGH** or **SINK** has several advantages. Using a container means rock garden plants can be grown anywhere, including on a patio or balcony. The plants are raised for easier viewing and working, and some difficult alpines which often rot in the garden can survive the winter in the excellent drainage provided by a deep trough. Many attractive types are available — look for an adequate hole or holes at the bottom. Place the trough or sink on firm supports in a sunny spot and cover the drainage hole or holes with crocks. Fill to within 2 in. (5 cm) of the top with planting mixture (see Rock Garden on page 68) and wait a couple of weeks before planting. Avoid all rampant growers and place a 1 in. (2.5 cm) layer of stone chippings over the surface. Water regularly in dry weather — continue until water comes out of the drainage holes.

A **SCREE** in nature is an area of loose rock at the base of a gully or cliff. In this competition-free environment a number of alpines flourish. You can create a scree bed in a sunny spot in the garden, but it is a laborious job. Remove soil from the area and fill with an 8 in. (20 cm) layer of broken bricks or stones topped with a 2 in. (5 cm) layer of coarse sand or gravel. Add an 8 in. (20 cm) layer of scree compost (1 part topsoil, 1 part peat or leafmould and 3 parts grit or gravel) to bring the level to the surface. When planting shake off as much compost as you can from the roots — after planting place a 1 in. (2.5 cm) layer of chippings around the plants. A number of small stones bedded into the surface around the plants will improve the appearance. Recommended types are Aethionema, Androsace, Dianthus, Erinus, Erodium, Phlox, Sempervivum and Viola.

A **DRY-STONE WALL** is made without mortar. Soil or planting mixture is used to fill the spaces between the stones and in the cracks a wide range of rock garden plants can be grown. Consider this type of structure when you have to build a retaining wall against a bank. Use limestone, sandstone or the dry-walling type of reconstituted stone blocks. A foundation of rubble or concrete should be used and the stones should slope about 10° backwards. Plant rooted cuttings as you go, placing the specimens sideways. Pack the mixture around the roots and fill the space between the back of the stones and the front of the bank. Spray the wall with water when planting is finished — water in dry weather until the plants are established. Recommended plants are Alyssum, Aubretia, Dianthus, Helianthemum and Phlox — on a shady wall grow Arabis, Campanula and Saxifraga.

TUFA is a rock which can be used as a home for rock garden plants — roots will grow into it because it is porous and can hold more than its own weight of water. Although tufa is a form of magnesium limestone it is suitable for lime-hating plants. Insert the base of a piece of tufa into a bed or rockery — it will soak up water like a sponge. The rock is soft and can be drilled quite easily — make a series of downward-sloping holes 1½ in. (4 cm) wide and 4 in. (10 cm) deep. Free the roots of a small plant from compost and wrap them in moist toilet paper. Push the wrapped roots into a hole and fill the space with paving-crack planting mixture — see page 68. Water after planting and during dry spells.

CHAPTER 10

VEGETABLES

Growing vegetables by the traditional allotment method is one of the most laborious activities in the garden. There is ground to be cleared and dug each year, and some of it will need fertilizing and manuring. Plants have to be sown or transplanted and then there are jobs like thinning and weeding.

So why do people do it? Firstly, they want to harvest at the peak of tenderness and flavour instead of having to wait for maximum yields like the professional grower. You can also serve vegetables within an hour of picking and with sweet corn, beans and asparagus this can be a new taste experience. This flavour virtue of home-grown vegetables is not nearly as important as this description makes it sound — most gardeners let their crops reach maximum size before harvesting. Next, there is the money-saving angle — no fresh vegetables to buy in summer and lots to freeze for winter. Again, this sounds better than it is in practice. In order to be self-sufficient you would have to devote a great deal of space and time to your vegetable plot. These days there are pick-your-own farms all round the country, so bulk supplies can be gathered quite cheaply without the effort of growing them.

This leaves just two worthwhile reasons for growing some vegetables in the easy-care garden. Above all there is the satisfaction of raising your own food — the thrill of watching the plants grow until they reach the plate in the dining room. The second unique attraction is that you can grow vegetables which you cannot readily buy in the shops — Welsh onion, Hamburg parsley etc.

These advantages of growing vegetables at home make it worthwhile for most gardeners, but you should follow the easy-care route if the work of traditional vegetable growing does not appeal to you. First of all, restrict the area to manageable proportions. Avoid long rows of plants — on pages 72–73 you can read about alternatives which are easier to look after. By far the most important of these alternatives is the bed method — no digging, much less weeding and higher yields per sq. metre.

There is no doubt that growing in beds rather than long rows is the best way to raise vegetables, but the choice of easy-care varieties is much trickier. It is generally agreed that peas, Brussels sprouts, cauliflowers and celery are best avoided, but this is not a hard-and-fast rule. That leaves quite an extensive list of easy-care ones as set out on pages 74–75, but even these involve the chore of annual sowing or transplanting. There are a few perennial vegetables for year after year picking — it is surprising that these are not more widely grown.

CHOOSE THE RIGHT METHOD

The Golden Rule

Vegetables are notoriously hard work and would seem to have no place in the easy-care garden. There are, however, two methods which do not involve hard work each year — the one to choose for worthwhile yields is the bed method.

The **ALLOTMENT METHOD** is the standard way and for most gardeners the only method of growing vegetables. The whole of the plot is cultivated and the plants are grown in rows. Strips of bare earth are left between each row or group of rows so that the gardener can walk along for watering, cultivating, picking etc. By the allotment method the longest beans and the heaviest potatoes are produced, but it is extremely laborious. There is the chore of digging each autumn and both the bare pathways and the large spaces left between the plants encourage weeds. In addition the long rows often result in a glut so that not all the produce can be used.

The **COTTAGE GARDEN METHOD** is the best way to grow vegetables if you don't want to devote a separate area of ground to them. They are planted among the flowers, bulbs, roses and shrubs in the mixed beds and borders. Ordinary vegetables can be grown, of course, but there are some types which are ornamental as well as useful. There is the red-veined ruby chard or the red-leaved beetroot and lettuce 'Lollo-Rossa'. Best of all are the climbing beans — scarlet runners or the purple-podded French ones.

The **CONTAINER METHOD** is the best way to grow vegetables if you don't have a garden. Any tub, pot or trough which is deeper than 8 in. (20 cm) can be used, but the favourite container these days is the growing bag. All sorts of vegetables apart from the bulky ones like Brussels sprouts, broccoli etc can be grown, but there is little point in growing 'ordinary' ones. Choose unusual or decorative ones, or grow rather tender vegetables such as aubergine, capsicum or tomato against a sheltered south-facing wall. Still, there are no rules and many people who do not bother with a vegetable plot use a variety of pots and bags to grow salad crops.

The **BED METHOD** is the best way to grow vegetables if you want an appreciable amount of produce. Yields are higher than you would obtain by the allotment method, but the size of each harvested vegetable is usually smaller. The reason for the high yields is that each vegetable is sown or planted in a block so that all the plants are the same distance from each other — the spacing is quite close so that the leaves of adjacent plants touch when the plants are mature. There are several distinct advantages. General maintenance is much easier — closely-planted vegetables smother most weeds and there are no muddy walkways between rows. Perhaps the important advantage is the removal of the need to dig every year.

GROWING VEGETABLES IN BEDS

The Golden Rule

Converting your vegetable plot to the bed method will mean some effort and perhaps some money, but in future years you will have much less work to do.

The basic principle is to create a series of rectangular beds devoted to vegetables. These beds are divided by permanent paths which are covered with gravel or bark chippings and the beds must be narrow enough so that all the plants can be reached from the path.

Construct the beds so that they run North–South if possible. Organic matter is added to the soil and it should be left to settle for at least a couple of weeks before sowing or planting. Sow short rows every 1–3 weeks if you want to avoid gluts.

The yearly round begins in autumn or early winter when a layer of organic matter such as rotted manure or garden compost is worked into the surface with a fork. Digging is not necessary as you have not trodden down the surface by walking on it.

Use the distances on pages 74–75 as your guide to the recommended spacing between plants after any thinning which may be necessary. If you are putting in transplants rather than sowing seed you can use the plastic mulch method — see the section on Mulching. Try not to grow the same vegetable in the bed year after year.

Bed Types

FLAT BEDS

The flat bed is the easiest type to create but you do need free-draining soil. Use the dimensions given for raised beds in the drawing below. Turn over the soil and work in a 1 in. (2.5 cm) layer of organic matter.

RAISED BEDS

10 ft (3 m) maximum

4 ft (1.2 m)

1½ ft (45 cm)

2–3 ft (60–90 cm)

Pathway covered with gravel or coarse bark chippings. Put black plastic sheeting underneath to prevent weed growth

The raised bed is the type to create if drainage is poor and the ground gets waterlogged in winter. You will have to build retaining walls — see the drawing above. Railway sleepers, bricks or blocks can be used but 1 in. (2.5 cm) thick pressure-treated wooden planks attached to 2 in. (5 cm) square corner posts are the usual choice. The raised bed should be at least 4 in. (10 cm) high — fork over the bottom and then fill with a mixture of 2 parts topsoil and 1 part organic matter.

CHOOSE EASY-CARE TYPES

The Golden Rule

You can grow nearly all the popular vegetables by the bed method, but it is better to stick to dwarf varieties of the easy ones. Consider growing perennial vegetables which do not need sowing or transplanting every year.

Easy-care Vegetables
PERENNIALS

NAME	NOTES
ASPARAGUS	Asparagus is not usually listed as an easy crop — free-draining soil, ample space and thorough bed preparation are necessary. Once established, however, it is easy to care for. Plant 1-year-old crowns 8 in. (20 cm) deep and 15 in. (37.5 cm) apart
EGYPTIAN ONION	The Egyptian or tree onion is an unusual plant which produces small onions instead of flowers on 3 ft (90 cm) stalks. Plant bulbils 9 in. (22.5 cm) apart in well-drained soil in late summer — picking time is June–January
RHUBARB	Usually regarded as a 'fruit' but is really a vegetable. Plant sets (pieces of crown) in February–March — bud should be just below surface and plants set at 3 ft (90 cm) intervals. Pick in April–July
SEAKALE	Reputed to be fussy, but seakale will grow in any ordinary soil. Plant thongs (root cuttings) in March — set them 18 in. (45 cm) apart and 2 in. (5 cm) deep. In November cover each plant with a pot or bucket. Cut in April, cook like asparagus
WELSH ONION	The Welsh or Japanese bunching onion is an excellent evergreen substitute for spring onions. Clumps of 2 ft (60 cm) high hollow leaves are produced — cut as required. Sow seed thinly in March — thin to 9 in. (22.5 cm) spacings

ANNUALS & BIENNIALS

NAME	SOW	DEPTH	PLANT	DISTANCE BETWEEN PLANTS	HARVEST	TIME TAKEN (weeks)
BEAN, BROAD	February –April	2 in. (5 cm)	—	6 in. (15 cm)	July –August	16S → H
	Favourite varieties include 'Aquadulce' and 'Bunyard's Exhibition' — the favourite dwarf is 'The Sutton'. Begin picking when pods are 3 in. (7.5 cm) long — cook whole					
BEAN, FRENCH	May –June	2 in. (5 cm)	—	6 in. (15 cm)	July –September	10S → H
	The popular Flat-podded or English varieties tend to become stringy as they mature. The Pencil-podded or Continental varieties (e.g 'Sprite') are stringless					
BEETROOT	April –June	1 in. (2.5 cm)	—	3 in. (7.5 cm)	June –October	11S → H
	Grow a globe variety — harvest when no larger than a tennis ball. Reliable varieties include 'Boltardy', 'Monopoly' and 'Monodet'					
CALABRESE	April –May	½ in. (1 cm)	June –July	15 in. (37.5 cm)	August –September	15S → H
	Grown for its green spears. 'Express Corona' is a good choice — the first heads are ready for cutting 45–50 days after planting out					

NAME	SOW	DEPTH	PLANT	DISTANCE BETWEEN PLANTS	HARVEST	TIME TAKEN (weeks)
CARROT	March –July	½ in. (1 cm)	—	4 in. (10 cm)	July –October	14S → H
	Pick a quick-maturing short-rooted variety such as the round 'Early French Frame' or the finger-long 'Amsterdam Forcing'					
COURGETTE	May –June	1 in. (2.5 cm)	—	18 in. (45 cm)	July –September	10S → H
	Courgettes are marrows cut at the immature stage when 3–4 in. (7.5–10 cm) long. Varieties include 'Gold Rush' (yellow) and 'Defender' (green)					
KALE	May	½ in. (1 cm)	July	15 in. (37.5 cm)	December	30S → H
	'Pentland Brig' is the variety to grow. Pick young leaves in winter, young shoots in early spring and spears (cook like broccoli) a little later					
LETTUCE	March –July	½ in. (1 cm)	—	9 in. (22.5 cm)	June –October	12S → H
	Grow a Miniature e.g 'Tom Thumb' or 'Little Gem' or a loose-leaf variety (e.g 'Salad Bowl') —a few leaves can be removed each time over many weeks					
ONION	—	Tip showing	March –April	3 in. (7.5 cm)	August	20P → H
	Grow sets rather than seed — harvest 2 weeks after stems topple over. Popular varieties include 'Stuttgarter Giant' and 'Sturon'					
POTATO	—	5 in. (12.5 cm)	March –April	12 in. (30 cm)	June –July	13P → H
	Grow an early variety for new potatoes in early summer — examples include 'Arran Pilot', 'Foremost', 'Pentland Javelin' and 'Sharpe's Express'					
RADISH	March –July	½ in. (1 cm)	—	2 in. (5 cm)	May –September	6S → H
	Nothing is easier to grow. There are many varieties — e.g 'Cherry Belle' (round/red), 'Sparkler' (round/white-red) and 'Large White Icicle' (long/white)					
SPINACH BEET	April	1 in. (2.5 cm)	—	8 in. (20 cm)	August –November	15S → H
	This type of leaf beet is similar to spinach but it is not prone to bolting and the leaves are larger and fleshier					
TOMATO	—	—	June	18 in. (45 cm)	August –September	12P → H
	An easy crop, but only if you choose a bush variety such as 'The Amateur' and grow it in a warm, sunny and sheltered spot					
TURNIP	March –June	½ in. (1 cm)	—	6 in. (15 cm)	May –September	10S → H
	Early or bunching varieties (e.g 'Snowball') are sown early in the year and picked at golf-ball size for salads or stews					

KEY
DISTANCE BETWEEN PLANTS

These spacings are the recommended distances between mature plants grown by the bed method. See a standard textbook (e.g The Vegetable Expert) or the seed packet for row and plant spacings for vegetables grown by the allotment method.

TIME TAKEN (weeks)
- **S** : Sowing
- **P** : Planting
- **→** : to
- **H** : Harvest

Broad Bean 'Aquadulce'

Onion 'Stuttgarter Giant'

HERBS

The use of herbs when cooking meat, fish, poultry, omelettes etc is now much more commonplace than it used to be, and no longer does the home cook feel restricted to mint, parsley, thyme and sage. Dried herbs are generally a poor substitute for fresh material, and fortunately the popular varieties are easy-care plants.

Herb growing is for everyone. If you don't have a garden or if open ground is short you can grow pots of chervil, marjoram, mint, parsley and thyme on the windowsill. Outdoors you can grow them in a mixed bed or border as in the cottage gardens of old. Best of all, however, is a raised herb bed. It is a good idea to grow them in compartments separated by permanent dividers of brick, wood, concrete slabs etc.

The standard requirements are some sun during the day, a well-drained soil, fairly regular picking to keep the plant compact and the replacement of perennials every three or four years. Most types can be raised from seed but it is better to buy them as small plants in pots from the garden centre. With shrubby herbs such as rosemary you will need only a single plant, but with smaller herbaceous types such as parsley you will require several specimens.

Construct the herb garden as close as practical to the house — herb gathering tends to be neglected in wet weather when the bed is situated at the far end of the garden. A herb garden can be bought for the patio (see page 77) in which various herbs are planted in the compartments.

Easy-care Herbs

NAME	NOTES
BASIL	Basil is only a temporary plant in the herb garden. Plant this annual in late May and pick leaves in summer as required. Height 9 in. (22.5 cm), spacing 12 in. (30 cm). An essential ingredient in many Italian recipes — the traditional partner is the tomato
CHERVIL	This ferny-leaved hardy herb grows quickly and the aniseed-flavoured leaves can be picked all year round. Height 15 in. (37.5 cm), spacing 9 in. (22.5 cm). The flavour is lost by cooking — add chopped leaves to soups, fish etc just before serving
CHIVES	One of the basic plants in the herb garden — its grass-like stems can be cut from March to October to give a mild onion flavour to many dishes. Height 12 in. (30 cm), spacing 9 in. (22.5 cm). Remove flower buds before they open
DILL	A tall annual with attractive feathery leaves and flat seed-heads in July. Pick leaves for immediate use or for drying. Height 24 in. (60 cm), spacing 12 in. (30 cm). The leaves are used as a garnish or in cooking fish dishes
FENNEL	This perennial has blue-green feathery foliage and a stronger aniseed flavour than dill. Pick leaves in summer as required. Height 48 in. (120 cm). Use the chopped leaves for salads, fish, vegetables and soups

NAME	NOTES
MARJORAM	Sweet marjoram is an annual — grow the perennial pot marjoram. Cut back dead stems in winter and pick leaves from spring to autumn. Height 15 in. (37.5 cm). Chopped leaves are sprinkled over meat or poultry before roasting
MINT	This robust invasive perennial is one of our favourite herbs. There are several varieties —spearmint is the popular one. Height 18 in. (45 cm), spacing 9 in. (22.5 cm). Many uses — mint sauce, summer drinks, new potatoes etc
PARSLEY	The deeply-divided leaves provide our most popular garnish. Pick regularly to ensure a continuous supply. Height 9 in. (22.5 cm), spacing 9 in. (22.5 cm). Use for decoration and also in white sauces and omelettes
ROSEMARY	An evergreen shrub with narrow leaves — give it a sheltered spot. Trim to 24 in. (60 cm) and in spring remove any shoots killed by frost. Becomes leggy — renew every 3 years. Traditional flavouring for lamb, pork and veal
SAGE	An attractive bush with violet flowers. Dry leaves in late spring for winter use. Height 24 in. (60 cm). Gather leaves regularly — renew every 3 years. Sage and its partner onion make a traditional poultry stuffing
SAVORY	Winter savory is a low-growing evergreen perennial with narrow leaves and tubular flowers. Height 9 in. (22.5 cm) — trim back in spring. Use in salads or egg dishes or as a substitute for sage when making stuffing
TARRAGON	French tarragon is an herbaceous perennial which is an invasive spreader like mint. Pick during summer — remove flowering shoots. Height 24 in. (60 cm). Widely used in French cooking, especially chicken and fish dishes
THYME	A low-growing aromatic shrub which can be picked all year round — flavour depends on the variety grown. Height 9 in. (22.5 cm), spacing 12 in. (30 cm). Many uses — traditional partner for parsley for stuffing as well as for rubbing over meat before roasting

FRUIT

It is impossible to generalise about fruit as an easy-care group of plants. A few are no more trouble than any straightforward ornamental tree or shrub, but others involve a lot of hard work if you are to get a worthwhile crop from healthy plants. It is of course worth a little trouble to pick your own produce for freezing, storing or eating straightaway, but the large number of pick-your-own farms throughout the country makes it less necessary nowadays to grow your own if you want lots of fruit for jam-making or preserving.

Consider first the tree fruits — apples, pears, plums, cherries, peaches etc. In this whole group only apples can be regarded as an easy-care crop, and then only if you choose with care. Pick the wrong variety and pollination may not take place or spraying will be necessary — pick the wrong rootstock and the tree will rapidly get out of hand. Pears require better growing conditions and are less reliable, cherries provide bird food unless the trees are netted and the plum crop is often lost to frost or bullfinches.

Most types of soft fruit require attention — during the year there is a need to feed, spray, prune, stake etc and worst of all is the need for protection against birds. Maincrop strawberries are by far the most popular soft fruit, but slugs and birds will attack the fruits every year and virus infection will make replanting essential every 3 or 4 years. Do not let this put you off strawberries completely — growing these plants in containers can solve the slug problem and growing an alpine variety overcomes the bird problem as the tiny fruits are rarely attacked. Gooseberries are not difficult but birds can once again be a problem. Blackcurrants are grown mainly for pies or jam-making and are not really worth the space and effort, but white and red currants are worth growing as they are an excellent ingredient for fruit salad and are not always available in the shops during the cropping season.

Autumn raspberries are the best of all the easy-care soft fruits. Unlike the popular summer ones they do not need attaching to wires and birds are seldom a problem. The main drawback is that yields are often disappointing. If supports are available blackberries are easy to grow and these days there are excellent thornless varieties to make picking easier.

The fruit situation can be summed up by saying that fruit has only a minor part to play in the easy-care garden as effort should generally go into ornamental plants rather than food crops. Unlike most vegetables, however, just a few plants can give a useful yield so look at the list overleaf before ruling them out.

CHOOSE EASY-CARE TYPES

Easy-care Fruits

APPLE

Rootstocks

Some rootstocks will produce dwarf trees, others create 20 ft (6 m) giants. Always check before you buy.

 ? M27 **✔ M9** **✔ M26** **✔ MM106**  **✘ MM111 & M2**

extremely dwarfing	**very dwarfing**	**dwarfing**	**semi-dwarfing**	**vigorous**
Bush only 6 ft (1.8 m) high after 15 years, but needs good soil and management.	Good choice for dwarf bush or cordon, but needs good soil and permanent staking.	Good choice for small bush and average conditions. Cropping starts in 4 years.	Most popular one but needs space — bush reaches 15 ft (4.5 m) at maturity.	Top yields, but trees are too tall and too wide for an easy-care garden.

Types

 ✔ BUSH **✘ STANDARD** **? CORDON** **✔ COMPACT COLUMN**

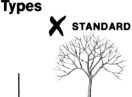  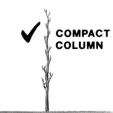

Most popular type — bushes have an open centre and a short trunk (dwarf bushes 1½–2 ft/45–60 cm — bushes 2–2½ ft/60–75 cm). Soon come into fruit and are easy to maintain. Mature size depends on rootstock — see above. Not suitable for planting in the lawn as branches are low.

Large trees grown on vigorous rootstocks. They are grown where there is plenty of space and high yields are required. The standard tree has a 6–7 ft (1.8–2.1 m) trunk — the half standard trunk is 4–4½ ft (1.2–1.4 m) high. These trees are difficult to care for.

A single-stemmed tree which is planted at 45° and tied to a permanent support system such as a fence. A dwarfing rootstock is used and vigorous varieties are avoided. Cordons are a good way of growing several varieties together in a restricted space but pruning is tricky.

Simplest type to look after — there is a single main stem with very few side branches, so little or no pruning is necessary. Ballerina type has varieties with indifferent flavours. The Minarette type grows to a similar height (6 ft/1.8 m) but offers well-known varieties such as James Grieve.

Varieties

A few varieties (e.g Arthur Turner and James Grieve) do not need a pollination partner, but others do and so it is wise to plant at least two different varieties when growing apples.

NAME	NOTES
ARTHUR TURNER	Large fruit. Picking August–September
DISCOVERY	Medium fruit. Picking August–September
JAMES GRIEVE	Medium fruit. Picking September
KATY	Small fruit. Picking September
SUNSET	Small fruit. Picking October–December

Pruning

The traditional method of training and pruning an apple tree is complicated, but there is a simple technique for the easy-care garden. In winter cut out dead wood and any branch which crosses over and touches others. Then remove a couple of the longest branches and those which are growing into other plants.

BLACKBERRY

A modern blackberry variety can be used as an ornamental climber as well as a provider of fruit for the kitchen. Flowers open in May–July and the cropping time is August–September.

Varieties

Grow a thornless variety. Choose Loch Ness for stout stems which require little or no support — yields are good and the fruit are large. Oregon Thornless has easily-trained canes which bear deeply-divided leaves.

Pruning

After picking cut out all the stems which have borne fruit, leaving this season's growth to fruit next year.

RASPBERRY

Autumn raspberries are easier to grow than the more popular summer-fruiting ones, but yields are generally lower and they do not thrive in cold districts. Fruit are borne on the tips of the canes produced this year.

Varieties

The one to grow is Autumn Bliss — it outyields all other autumn varieties and the picking season lasts from August to October. The fruit is bright red and the stems do not require support.

Pruning

Pruning could not be easier — simply cut off all the stems to ground level in early spring.

RED CURRANT

Red currants make an attractive garnish for desserts, but they are too tart to serve on their own and so are used for pies, jams etc. Grow as an open-centred goblet-shaped bush — the shiny fruit will be ready for picking in July.

Varieties

There are two varieties from which to make your choice. Laxton's No.1 is an old favourite which bears heavy crops. Red Lake is later but the fruit are larger and growth is less vigorous.

Pruning

After picking cut out thin drooping branches and any old ones crowding the centre of the bush.

STRAWBERRY

Birds, slugs, disease etc make strawberries a difficult crop if you have little time to spare, but a strawberry barrel (see The Container Expert) can be an attractive feature. In beds or borders grow either perpetual or alpine ones.

Varieties

Look for Aromel, Gento and Rapella (perpetual varieties) or Baron Solemacher (alpine). Grow as a border edging for late summer-autumn fruit — birds leave alpine strawberries alone.

Pruning

Grow alpine varieties as annuals — with perpetuals remove old leaves when picking is over.

WHITE CURRANT

Unlike its red cousin the fruit are sweet with a grape-like flavour. Growth habit is similar and birds may take some of the crop. In the easy-care garden you can grow a bush or two in a mixed border or as part of an informal hedge.

Varieties

Only one variety is readily available. White Versailles bears long and heavy trusses of pale yellow fruit from early July onwards. It is reliable and should give good crops year after year.

Pruning

After picking cut out thin drooping branches or any old ones crowding the centre of the bush.

CHAPTER 12

THE GREENHOUSE

A greenhouse can be a joy if you have a love of growing plants and have time to spare. There are bedding plants to raise from seed, cuttings to root, half-hardy perennials to keep over winter and tender vegetables to cultivate. In addition a greenhouse is a cosy retreat which separates you from your workaday worries as well as from the weather.

Unfortunately we must stop there. If money is no problem then a fully automated greenhouse can be installed, but for nearly everyone greenhouse growing is very much a manual operation and is perhaps the most labour-intensive of all aspects of gardening.

The major problem is the need for daily watering and for the regular opening and shutting of ventilators during the summer months. There are insects to keep in check and glass panes to shade, and care at holiday time calls for a kindly and knowledgeable friend or relative nearby.

So only buy a greenhouse if you have money to spare, enough free time to care for it properly and a desire to grow things which need the protection of glass. Buy a book on greenhouse growing and read it carefully if you are new to the subject — you cannot leave things to nature as you can so often outdoors.

To buy or not to buy is not the question for many easy-care gardeners. At least one in every ten families already have a greenhouse, and many of them just do not have the time or the inclination to look after it. The result is depressingly common. By the end of the summer there are a few bedraggled tomato plants which have struggled through in infrequently-watered growing bags, and a collection of pots, trays, garden tools etc.

It needn't be that way. Provided you are not over-ambitious you can grow a range of plants successfully in an easy-care way. The first step is to bring in some simple automation and this need not mean a lot of money or trouble. You will need a form of simple watering system and one or more automatic ventilators to remove the need for daily attention. Secondly, choose plants which do not need a lot of looking after, and finally pot up plugs (see page 54) rather than sowing seeds when raising bedding plants for planting outdoors in spring.

Your decision to grow plants under glass may be a desire to have flowering plants around you in the dull days between autumn and spring. In this case you might well be better off with a conservatory than a greenhouse. Here you can have the number of pots that you can comfortably manage by following the rules of house plant care — the rest of the space is filled with furniture.

CHOOSE THE RIGHT GREENHOUSE

The Golden Rule

The usual advice given to the easy-care gardener is not to buy a greenhouse. However, some busy people are willing to find the time to grow things under glass. When choosing a model make sure that it is made of low-maintenance material and do not aim to create hothouse conditions.

SIZE

If time but not space is short you might be tempted to buy a tiny greenhouse as there would be less to look after. You would be wrong — it is much more difficult to control the temperature and avoid draughts in a small house than in a larger one. A good choice for the average garden is an 8 ft x 6 ft (2.4 m x 1.8 m) house — check that it has at least one roof ventilator and one side ventilator.

MATERIAL

Many people consider wood to be the most attractive material, but cheap softwoods may rot after a few years. There are rot-proof woods (teak, western red cedar etc) but they are more expensive than aluminium, the most popular frame material. It loses slightly more heat at night than wood but its drawbacks are minor. The latest material is unplasticised PVC — quite expensive but no maintenance is needed.

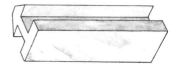

HEATING

✔ **COLD GREENHOUSE**
Unheated except by the sun

minimum temperature 28°F (–2°C)
when outside temperature falls to 20°F (–7°C)
Overall benefits: Plants are protected from wind, rain and snow
Growth is approximately 3–4 weeks ahead of outdoor plants
Drawbacks: No growth occurs in the depths of winter
Unsuitable for overwintering frost-sensitive plants

•

? **COOL GREENHOUSE**
Heater required during the cooler months

minimum temperature 45°F (7°C)
Overall benefits: Plants are protected from wind, rain, snow and frost
Growth is approximately 3–4 weeks ahead of cold greenhouse plants
Minimum temperature is just high enough to support plant growth
Frost-sensitive plants can be overwintered
Drawback: Some form of heating is required between autumn and spring

•

✗ **WARM GREENHOUSE**
Heater required during most months

minimum temperature 55°F (13°C)
Overall benefits: A wide range of plants can be grown during the winter months
Exotic flowers and fruits can be planted
Drawback: Fuel costs are about three times higher than cool greenhouse costs

INSTALL EASY-CARE EQUIPMENT

The Golden Rule

Greenhouse gardening is a daily chore in summer if you do not have some form of automatic watering and automatic ventilation. Some systems are expensive, but low-priced effective versions are available.

Automatic Watering

There are several ways of making watering easier — the **automatic** ones work from the mains either directly through a tap or indirectly through a reservoir tank. All the plants are kept watered until the system is switched off. This switching on and off is usually done by hand, but you can buy a simple timer or a complex water computer which can be set to give watering periods of various lengths on different days. Nearly all amateur set-ups are much simpler and are **semi-automatic** — the reservoirs have to be filled with water manually and may need switching on every time water is required.

Water computer

SAND BENCH

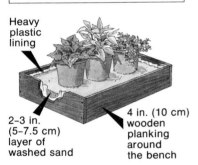

Heavy plastic lining

2–3 in. (5–7.5 cm) layer of washed sand

4 in. (10 cm) wooden planking around the bench

The sand (or capillary) bench has been around for many years, but it has never become popular. The staging holding the tray must be level and stout. The sand is kept moist by means of a watering can or a pipe connected to a manually-filled reservoir or header tank. Plastic (not clay) pots without crocks are screwed into the moist sand.

CAPILLARY MATTING

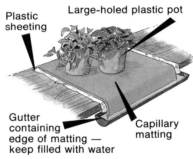

Plastic sheeting

Large-holed plastic pot

Gutter containing edge of matting — keep filled with water

Capillary matting

A modern alternative to the sand bench — lighter, easier to install and more popular, but it has to be replaced after a time as it becomes clogged with algae. Polythene sheeting is laid on the bench and the matting is placed on top of it — this is kept permanently moist by means of a watering can, pipe fed from a tank, or a water-filled gutter.

TRICKLE IRRIGATION

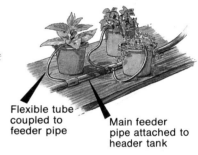

Flexible tube coupled to feeder pipe

Main feeder pipe attached to header tank

Greatly favoured by commercial growers, but an unsightly technique for a display greenhouse. The main pipe is fed from a header tank and small pipes wind from this in spaghetti-like fashion to exit points inserted in each pot. Water trickles into each pot either continuously or on a time-controlled basis. Check frequently for blockages.

Automatic Ventilation

There are times when a series of rapid air changes is necessary within the greenhouse. If the temperature rises above 80°F (27°C) or the humidity approaches 100 per cent it is essential to have about 40–60 air changes per hour. An automatic ventilator may be described as an 'optional extra' in the catalogue, but it is a vital piece of equipment if you cannot spare the time to go out daily to open and close the ventilators by hand. It is a non-electrical item which has a tube containing a heat-expanding compound as the control unit. A plunger within the tube moves as the temperature changes, and this opens or closes the ventilator. Extractor fans are noisy and quite expensive to run — they are not usually necessary unless the house is a large one.

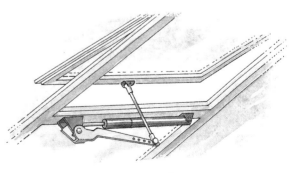

Automatic ventilator

CHOOSE EASY-CARE TYPES

The greenhouse enthusiast will often choose plants which offer a challenge — the exotic orchid like Cattleya, the tropical beauty like Gardenia and the time-consuming fruit such as the Black Hamburgh grape. For the easy-care gardener the greenhouse is used in a different way. First of all there are bedding plants to raise, which means saving both money at planting time and the effort involved in bringing home fully-grown specimens from the garden centre. Then there are tomatoes which have long been the most popular greenhouse crop — but there are other tender ones such as Aubergine and Capsicum which you can try. The story need not end there. Pots of strawberries can be brought into the cool greenhouse from the garden in January for picking in April. There are pots of late-flowering Chrysanthemums to bring under glass in late September. The list could go on — easy orchids such as Phalaenopsis, greenhouse bulbs such as the Spider Lily and so on, but you must avoid at all costs having too many different sorts of plants if you want to refrain from being a slave to your greenhouse.

ORNAMENTALS

If you have a cool greenhouse (see page 84) rather than a cold one then scores of house plants which are available from your garden centre can be grown there at the appropriate season of the year. Examples include Bougainvillea, Amaryllis, Lachenalia, Zantedeschia, Asparagus Fern, Callistemon, Campanula, Chrysanthemum, Cineraria, Gerbera, Hydrangea, Kalanchoe, Pelargonium and Salpiglossis.

BEDDING PLANTS

Don't begin from seed — germination requires a higher temperature than that needed for the growth of seedlings. It is better and easier to buy tiny plants ('plugs') in April or May and put them into small pots of compost. Keep in a cool greenhouse until planting out time in late May or early June. Make sure that the plants are hardened off by exposing them gradually to outdoor conditions before the final move into the garden.

TOMATOES

Grow a bush variety (e.g Minibel, Red Alert, Totem) rather than a cordon tomato — the 1–3 ft (30–90 cm) high plants need little or no training, de-shooting or stopping. Buy seedlings rather than trying to raise your own from seed and plant out when the first flower truss is just beginning to open. In a cold house this should be in late April/early May for picking to start in July.

CHAPTER 13

BEATING THE TIME WASTERS

For the person who has read the standard textbooks and follows the traditional cultural techniques without question it can seem that looking after the garden is a round of tiring and rather boring jobs. The round begins with digging over flower beds and the vegetable plot at the start of the year and then seed sowing as the soil warms up. There is planting out in the spring which is followed by regular weeding and then the chore of daily watering of beds and containers during the long dry spells in summer. At the end of the season there is pruning to do, and most books make this sound like a complex process involving a number of precise cuts.

In this chapter these hard-work tasks have been grouped together as the time wasters — a concept which will cause many a dedicated and successful gardener to splutter in protest. 'Time waster' does overstate the case against these techniques, but there is still a case to answer. All too often digging, weeding, watering and pruning are slavishly undertaken when they are either not necessary or could be replaced by alternative techniques which save effort.

These easy-care techniques are not for everyone — for millions of gardening enthusiasts the time wasters are the cornerstones of their activity in caring for beds, borders, lawns and containers. They would quite rightly point out that there are occasions when each one — digging, weeding, watering and pruning are essential, but an important appeal for them is that these jobs are both enjoyable and relaxing. Hard work, perhaps, but so are jogging, tennis and aerobics. These devotees do not need this book — there is a wealth of information in scores of excellent standard textbooks to show them what to do.

The purpose of this chapter is to describe the occasions when the classic time wasters are not necessary and can occasionally do more harm than good. This will be welcome news for all those people who do not find the strenuous routine jobs of gardening enjoyable or have neither the time nor perhaps the health to allow them to do so much work.

It must be stressed that the easy-care approach is not the same thing as neglect. Leave the vegetable plot undug, let the weeds in beds and borders run wild, leave the annuals and newly-planted shrubs unwatered during periods of prolonged drought and let invasive perennials spread unchecked in the rockery and the result will be an unattractive eyesore. An attractive easy-care garden can only be achieved by making some of the design changes described on pages 12–15 and moving over to easy-care plants instead of relying on ones needing regular pruning, spraying or lifting at the end of the growing season. It is then necessary to use a number of work-saving techniques to reduce the effort spent on the time wasters described in this chapter.

DIGGING

Any general gardening book will list the merits of digging the vegetable plot or flower bed. The upper layer of soil is broken up and clods are exposed to the elements. Compost or manure can be incorporated and annual weeds are buried. In addition the roots of perennial weeds are exposed and can be removed. The problems with digging are sometimes not mentioned. Dig at the wrong time and you can harm the soil — dig in the wrong way and you can harm yourself. In shallow soil there is the real danger of burying the fertile top few inches and bringing up infertile clay or sand.

You should follow a no-dig programme. This consists of an initial turning over of the soil by digging if the ground has not been cultivated before or if the soil in an established plot is heavy and has been badly compacted. After that the annual treatment should be a no-dig programme which will build up the fertility over the years.

STEP ONE DIG ONCE IF YOU HAVE TO — AND DO IT PROPERLY

Dig only if the soil is in bad condition. When digging it is essential to put a layer of organic matter at the bottom of the trench before turning over the soil to fill it. This trench must never be deep enough to bring up a subsoil of clay, chalk or sand.

1 Choose the right season — early winter for most soils and early spring for light land. Choose the right day — the ground should be moist but not water-logged nor frozen

2 Wear clothes that are warm — you should not be uncomfortably hot nor cold when digging. Make sure your back is fully covered and wear stout shoes

3 Use the right equipment — a spade for general work or a fork if the soil is very heavy or stony. Carry a scraper and use it to keep the blade or prongs clean

4 Try to keep your back straight — avoid any sudden twists from the hips and on no account strain harder than you are used to doing at home or at work

5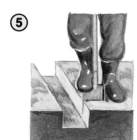
Drive in the spade vertically. Press (do not kick) down on the blade. This should be at right angles to the trench

6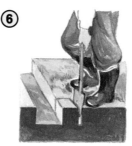
The next cut should be parallel to the trench, 6–8 in. (15–20 cm) behind the face. Do not take larger slices

7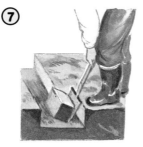
Pull steadily (do not jerk) on the handle so as to lever the soil on to the blade. Lift up the block of soil

8
With a flick of the wrist turn the earth into the trench in front — turn the spadeful right over to bury the weeds

9 Work for 10 minutes if you are reasonably fit but out of condition, then sit down or do a non-strenuous job until you feel rested. Work for 20 minutes between rests if you are fit and used to physical exercise. For most people 30 minutes digging is quite enough for the first day

Large Areas
Think twice before lifting a spade if you have a large area of hard and compacted earth to turn over. A typical example is the ground left by the builders. Hire a cultivator which can work to a depth of 8 in. (20 cm) or call in a contractor.

STEP TWO | CARRY OUT THE NO-DIG PROGRAMME EACH YEAR

The no-dig method of gardening is not a no-work system. It does save you the back-aching job of digging the vegetable garden and the flower beds every year, but it may involve some redesign work and will certainly involve an organic dressing over the surface every year. The benefits can be remarkable. The uppermost layer of soil is the most fertile and this is not buried by digging — an important point with shallow-rooting annuals. The weed problem may be greatly reduced and so is the need to water in dry weather, and both soil fertility and structure are steadily improved by the regular application of organic matter.

There are two fundamental requirements if you are to obtain these benefits. First of all you must make sure that soil compaction due to regular treading down during the season is kept to an absolute minimum. This means that you will need a design whereby the plants can be tended without you having to tread on the ground around them. Secondly an annual mulch has to be applied each year.

1 The average person can reach about 2 ft (60 cm) across a bed for planting, weeding etc without having to step on to the soil. In order to avoid compaction your beds for vegetables and annuals will need some form of edging or permanent pathways every 4 ft (1.2 m). The ideal answer is to create flat or raised beds with gravel, paving or shredded bark paths as described on page 73, but this is not essential. You can create permanent pathways of trodden down earth and carry out the no-dig programme in the beds between.

2 Once the growing season is over it is time to begin the no-dig programme. Everyone agrees that the soil should be moist and reasonably warm when the organic matter is applied, but there is some debate over the best time — late October or May. Perhaps the best plan is to put down the mulch in autumn if the ground is to be used for sowing seeds in spring and to spread the humus layer in May if the land is to be used for late May/early June bedding out. Before putting down this layer it is necessary to clean up the surface. Remove any debris and old plants and then tackle the weeds — see pages 90-92. Hand pull if only a few are present — hoe if there are more. Spray with glyphosate if there is a serious weed problem.

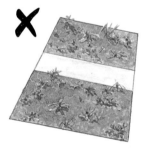
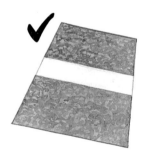

3 Lightly prick over the surface with a fork and then apply a layer of organic mulching material. Read the section on mulching beginning on page 96 — this technique is vital for easy-care gardening. If you do have a large area of beds and borders then obtaining sufficient organic material may seem to be a problem, but it shouldn't be. Don't think about buying peat or proprietary materials — make as much garden compost as you can and look for farms, stables etc which sell bags of well-rotted manure at a giveaway price. Making seed drills when the time arrives may be a little tricky — before you begin prick the humus layer into the surface soil if necessary.

WEEDING

In survey after survey weeding is rated as the most disliked of the time wasters. Digging is hard but for most gardeners it is a once a year job. Watering can be tedious, but outdoors it is generally just a dry-weather task. Weeding, however, is a season-long chore. In most gardens the job is tackled badly. Little is done to prevent an infestation around growing plants, and then we wait until the weeds are truly an eyesore. The gardener then spends hours hoeing, forking out and hand pulling with each bed in turn — only to find that the first bed is again full of weeds before the last bed or border is reached!

However clever you are there is no way of completely protecting your garden from weeds, but the easy-care gardener can do much better than the sorry tale above. The first task is to get to know a little about weeds — annual ones are treated differently from perennial ones. Next you must use one or two simple techniques to keep weeds away — prevention is always better than cure. Finally it is necessary to deal with the weeds which do appear as quickly as possible. In all cases the job must be undertaken before annual weeds produce seed and before perennial ones spread.

STEP ONE · GET TO KNOW A LITTLE ABOUT WEEDS

Weeds are not the outlaws of the plant world — they are simply wild flowers, grasses and sometimes garden plants (e.g self-seeded Alchemilla and Sycamore) growing where you don't want them to be. They give the garden a neglected look and compete for light, water and nutrients.

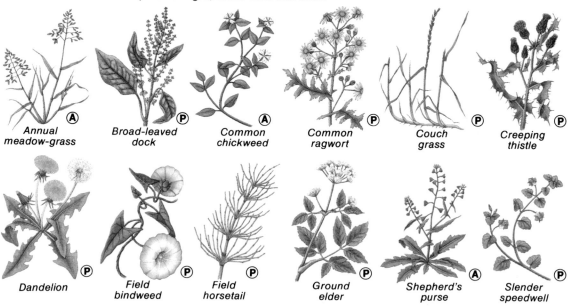

Annual meadow-grass (A)

Broad-leaved dock (P)

Common chickweed (A)

Common ragwort (P)

Couch grass (P)

Creeping thistle (P)

Dandelion (P)

Field bindweed (P)

Field horsetail (P)

Ground elder (P)

Shepherd's purse (A)

Slender speedwell (P)

Annual Weeds (A)

Annual weeds complete at least one life cycle from seed to seed during the season. They spread by seeding, and all fertile soils contain a large reservoir of annual weed seeds. The golden rule is that emerged annual weeds must be killed before they produce seeds — kill them by hand pulling, hoeing or burning off with a contact weedkiller.

Perennial Weeds (P)

Perennial weeds survive by means of under-ground stems or roots which act as storage organs over winter. Dig out the whole plant including the root if you can. Otherwise the leaves must be regularly removed to starve out the underground storage organs or else use a translocated weed-killer which will travel to the underground parts.

STEP TWO ## GET TO KNOW A LITTLE ABOUT WEEDKILLERS

A large collection of weedkillers (other name : herbicides) lines the shelves of garden centres and DIY stores in spring and summer. Many are based on the same active ingredients but there are still a number of basically different types. It is not the purpose of this page to bore you with all sorts of technical details, but you must have a basic knowledge of how these chemicals work if you are to avoid the twin dangers of killing garden plants and not harming the weeds. There is no single product which is safe on all plants and lethal to all weeds — you will have to pick and choose with care following the guidelines below.

Selective or Non-selective Action?

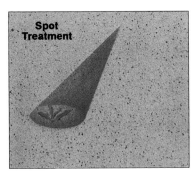

A **Selective Weedkiller** damages only a limited range of plants — use when the plants in question are resistant and most or all of the important weeds are susceptible. Example : lawn weedkillers.

A **Non-selective Weedkiller** damages garden plants as well as weeds — use on uncultivated land or choose a brand which can be applied by directed treatment (see below) around plants. Example : paraquat.

Contact or Systemic Action?

A **Contact Weedkiller** kills only those parts of the plant which are touched, so complete leaf cover is required. These products are fast-acting and are excellent for dealing with annual weeds, serving as a chemical hoe. But movement within the plant is either very limited or absent, so there is no long-lasting action against perennial weeds. Example : paraquat/diquat.

A **Residual Weedkiller** enters the plant through the roots. These products remain active in the soil for weeks or even years, depending on the chemical concentration, soil type etc. They tend to be unspectacular in action, killing the weeds below ground as they germinate. This chemical type is found in path weedkillers. Examples : simazine, dichlobenil, sodium chlorate, propachlor.

A **Translocated (Systemic) Weedkiller** moves in the sap stream, so roots as well as leaves are affected after spraying. Complete leaf cover is not required. These products are effective against many weeds, but action is often slow and the results are often governed by timing, weather etc. Examples : glyphosate, sodium chlorate, lawn weedkillers.

Spot or Overall Treatment?

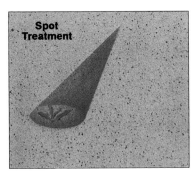

Spot Treatment

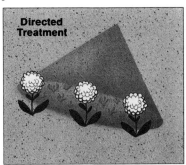

Directed Treatment

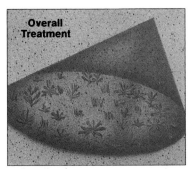

Overall Treatment

Application to a single weed or a group of weeds. Examples are painting the leaves of a perennial weed growing next to a rose with a translocated weedkiller such as glyphosate, and putting a pinch of lawn sand in the heart of a deep-rooted lawn weed. It is useful for dealing with isolated weeds not killed by a previous treatment.

Application to a group of weeds, great care being taken to avoid contact with nearby garden plants. Choose a still day and use a watering can fitted with a dribble bar. Examples are paraquat/diquat in the vegetable garden and glyphosate around herbaceous perennials and shrubs.

Application to the whole area which has a weed problem. The weedkiller may be a non-selective one where the area is either a path or land not being used for growing plants, or a selective weedkiller where the land contains plants which are resistant to the chemical — for example lawn weed-killers. Be careful to avoid drift outside the treated area.

STEP THREE | # PREVENT WEEDS APPEARING

The basic reason why you have a weed problem is bare ground. You can hoe or hand pull the weeds around growing plants and in some cases they can be safely sprayed, but if the soil is uncovered then the problem returns. Weed seeds on or near the surface and pieces of perennial weeds start to grow.

Digging is often an ineffectual way of controlling weeds on a long term basis. The annual types on the surface are buried, but a host of seeds are brought to the surface. With care some perennial weed roots can be removed, but all too often the roots of thistles, dandelions etc and the bulbs of oxalis and ground elder are spread around. The real answer is to try to cover the surface around plants in beds and borders. You can use a non-living cover (a mulch) or a living one (ground-cover plants).

Apply a mulch

One of the purposes of mulching (see pages 96–99) is to suppress the germination of weed seeds and to make easier the hand pulling of the ones which may appear. For weed control there are 2 basic types. The humus mulches such as bark, grass clippings etc will reduce the weed problem and the weed control ones such as black polyethylene, woven polypropylene and old carpeting will stop weed growth completely.

Use a residual weedkiller

The only popular type for the gardener is the path weedkiller which prevents weeds appearing in gravel, in cracks between stones etc. Seed germination is inhibited for a whole season. Residual weedkillers for use around fruit trees, roses etc are available, but they must be used with care.

Plant ground cover

Creeping evergreens with leafy stems provide an excellent way of suppressing weed growth on bare ground or banks etc and also around trees, shrubs and clumps of perennials. Establishing ground-cover plants as effective weed-controlling agents does take a little effort (see page 100) but this work is well worth while. With bedding plants you can solve the ground-cover problem by planting them closer together than usually recommended.

Bark-covered plastic sheeting

STEP FOUR | # GET RID OF WEEDS PROMPTLY

Weeds will appear in your beds and borders unless you use a sheeting form of mulch — see page 99. These weeds should be kept in check while they are still small. Hand pulling may be sufficient, especially if you have put down an organic mulch. If there are lots of weeds, however, you will have to use either a hoe or a weedkiller.

Pull by hand

The simplest method and still the right technique in certain situations. These situations include the removal of well-grown but easily-uprooted annual weeds in beds, the digging out of deep-rooted weeds in the lawn and the removal of weeds growing among the alpines in the rockery. With perennial weeds use a small fork to uproot them — don't pull up by the stems. Consider hand pulling where there are a few large weeds, but not where the problem is widespread and serious.

Use a contact or translocated weedkiller

Use a non-persistent contact weedkiller (see page 91) to get rid of annual weeds around plants and to burn off the tops of perennial ones. Apply glyphosate (a translocated weedkiller) to kill these perennial types. Make sure that the weeds are growing actively and remember that glyphosate works slowly — a second treatment may be necessary. For difficult weeds such as ground elder and bindweed paint the leaves with glyphosate gel.

Use a hoe

The hoe is the traditional enemy of the emerged weed, and despite all the advances of science it still remains the most popular method of killing weeds around growing plants. It is much quicker than hand pulling, and will kill large numbers of annual weeds if the soil surface is dry, the hoe blade is sharp and the depth of cut is kept shallow. Hoeing is not really effective against perennial weeds — use at regular intervals to starve out the roots.

Swan-necked hoe

PRUNING

Pruning worries most gardeners more than it should. Textbook instructions tend to be over-detailed and over-complex for the easy-care gardener, as previous chapters in this book illustrate. With roses (page 45) simply cut back hybrid teas, floribundas and patio roses by half in early spring — with other roses just give them a trim if necessary. Shrubs (page 37) and fruit trees (page 80) can also be dealt with quite simply. The thing you have to avoid is legginess and plants growing beyond the space you want to allow them. In both cases wood must be removed when flowering is over, and if you have neglected the job then removing a lot of branches may be necessary and so much or all of next season's bloom may be lost. So cut back the tallest leggiest branches at the recommended time and prune to stop overcrowding. Finally, two rules. If shrubs are too close then thinning out is better than constantly hacking back. Next, if a shrub has enough space then remember that too little pruning is better than too much. If in doubt, don't prune.

TYPES OF PRUNING

Shape Formation

This type of pruning is necessary for some types of young trees and shrubs — for example fruit trees, standard roses and topiary-cut evergreens. It sets the basic growth pattern — it can be done at home but for the easy-care gardener it is better to buy ready-shaped specimens from the nursery or garden centre.

Flower/Fruit Maintenance

This type of pruning is designed to ensure that both the quantity and quality of blossom will be maintained on well-shaped shrubs or trees. It is true that some shrubs (e.g Buddleia, Lilac, Tamarisk, Ribes, Potentilla, Spiraea japonica etc) need cutting back annually if they are not to grow into leggy unattractive plants, but nearly all easy-care types (pages 32–33) require little or no routine pruning every year.

Space Maintenance

This type of pruning gets little mention in many textbooks, but in the average garden it is more important than flower/fruit maintenance. Shrubs which have been planted too closely together grow into each other after a time, and if left for too long become misshapen. Having to cut back at this late stage can mean serious loss of flowers next season, so cut back at the first sign of a problem.

Health Maintenance

This type of pruning is important but is often neglected. During the dormant season all broken, dead and badly-diseased branches should be cut out. Prune back to healthy stain-free wood. Remove branches of variegated trees and shrubs which have reverted to bearing all-green foliage as soon as they are seen.

PRUNING TIPS

Large branches: Saw the branch flush with the trunk — do not leave snags. Do not attempt this task if the job is dangerous or difficult — call in a tree surgeon

The right piece of equipment depends on the thickness of the branch — see page 105. Always buy good quality tools and keep them clean and sharp

When lopping a large branch cut through a quarter of the way before sawing from the top

All cuts must be clean — pare off any ragged parts. Collect up all prunings — compost them if they are soft or burn them if woody or diseased

WATERING

The way that most people treat their plants during a prolonged dry spell is wrong. Not only does it involve a lot of effort but it can also do more harm than good in some cases. When the drought arrives the usual sequence of events is as follows. At first we do nothing, hoping that rain will fall in a day or two. It doesn't, and drought symptoms begin to appear on a few of the plants. The foliage turns dull and wilting takes place. Brown patches appear on the lawn. So we spring into action — the lawn sprinkler is used for a short time each day and we go around the garden with a watering can or hose to dampen the surface on a daily basis.

There are two basic errors — we try to water everything instead of the high-risk areas and we apply too little water too frequently. Soil with an average cover of plants loses about 4½ gallons of water per sq. yard (25 litres per sq.m) every week during the summer months. In the case of a prolonged drought the roots of a plant must be able to tap the soil reserves of water if rain has not fallen and the ground has not been watered. The ability of a plant to tap these reserves depends on a number of things — soil type, plant type, how long the specimen has been planted etc. The golden rule is not to try to water everything unless the garden is really small. To replace the soil reserves about 1 in. (2.5 cm) of rain or tap water has to fall on the surface. When watering it is essential that this water should not be applied in dribbles on a daily basis. This would result in rapid water loss by evaporation, development of surface roots which are damaged in hot weather, and germination of weed seeds.

Do not wait until the dry days of summer before you begin your battle against drought. Follow the plan on the next page. For lawns (page 25) and containers (page 58) there are special sets of rules.

THE HIGH-RISK PLANTS & AREAS

Risk higher than average. Water promptly and properly in times of drought — see page 95.

- **Bedding plants** for at least 6 weeks after planting
- **Hardy perennials** for the first year after planting
- **Shrubs** and **trees** for the first 1–2 years after planting
- Numerous **vegetables** — tomatoes, cucumbers, sweet corn, beans, peas, onions, marrows and celery
- Several **soft fruits** — strawberries and currants

- **Containers** — tubs, hanging baskets, window boxes, growing bags etc. See page 58
- **Sandy** and **low-humus** soils
- **Shallow-rooted plants**. Not all of these plants are small — some (e.g hydrangea, silver birch, rhododendron etc) are large shrubs or trees
- **Rain-shadow plants** — specimens growing within 2 ft (60 cm) of the house wall

THE LOW-RISK PLANTS

Risk lower than average. No need to water during periods of ordinary drought. If you decide to water, do it properly.

Achillea	Ceanothus	Dianthus	Iberis	Rosmarinus
Alyssum	Cistus	Euonymus	Lavandula	Sedum
Armeria	Convolvulus	Genista	Mahonia	Stachys
Artemisia	Cotoneaster	Grasses	Nepeta	Thymus
Buddleia	Cytisus	Helianthemum	Pyracantha	Yucca

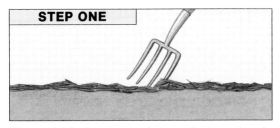

STEP ONE

Plants look lovely at the garden centre in summer, but wait until autumn if you can when the dry season will be over. Before planting build up the water-holding capacity by forking in plenty of humus-making material such as compost or manure — see Chapter 2 for details.

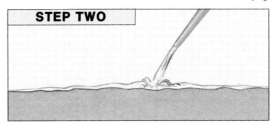

STEP TWO

The water reservoir in the soil should be reasonably full before you begin sowing or planting. This calls for watering thoroughly if the soil is dry — the ground should be moist to a depth of about 9 in. (22.5 cm). Now you are ready to start planting — follow the rules in Chapter 2.

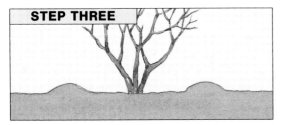

STEP THREE

Water gently but thoroughly to settle the soil around the roots. With large plants it is a good idea to create a water catchment area for any future watering which may be necessary. With shrubs and trees build a ridge of soil around the base to create a watering basin. With large herbaceous plants such as dahlias or tomatoes you should bury a large pot at planting time near to the base of the stem.

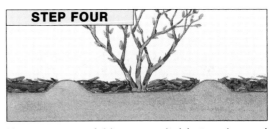

STEP FOUR

Now comes mulching — a vital but underused technique. The basic principle is to apply an organic layer of compost, well-rotted manure, bark chippings etc around the base of the plant when the soil is moist and reasonably warm. May is the best time, and this layer should be topped up if necessary each year. The ability of the plant to withstand drought is markedly increased — see pages 96-99 for details.

STEP FIVE

As noted in the list of high-risk plants on page 94 it is sometimes necessary to water newly-planted specimens. Look for the tell-tale signs of drought — dull foliage, wilting etc and then fill the watering basin or the pot (see Step 3 above) using 1–4 gallons (4.5–18 litres) depending on the size of plant, soil type and air temperature. With smaller plants or shrubs etc without a water catchment area apply the water overall at the rate of 2–4 gallons per sq. yard (11–22 litres per sq.m). Hold the watering can spout or hose nozzle close to the ground and water slowly — do not use a rose or spray nozzle unless you are watering bedding plants.

STEP SIX

It may be necessary to repeat the watering if rain does not fall — do not assume that a light summer shower will top up the water reserves in the soil. There is no easy way to determine the right time for this repeat watering — dig down with a trowel and examine the soil at 3–4 in. (7.5–10 cm) below the surface. It is time to water if it is dry. As a general rule watering is required every 5–7 days during a period of drought in summer — on no account should you water every couple of days because the plants continue to droop or are not growing. Only newly-planted ornamentals and a few vegetables should need watering if you have followed Steps 1–4.

CHAPTER 14

USING THE WORK SAVERS

MULCHING

Mulching really comes into its own in the easy-care garden. All mulches reduce the growth of weeds — some stop weed growth completely and the remainder make weed control a relatively simple matter. As shown below the humus mulch bestows a host of additional benefits — improved soil structure, less need to water in summer etc. Yet most gardeners do not mulch at all, and those who do generally misunderstand and underuse the technique. Basically a mulch is a layer of material placed around plants in order to improve the soil and plant growth and/or to suppress weed growth. In this section you will learn why, where, how and when to mulch.

The Humus Mulch

Humus mulches are bulky organic materials which improve the soil, stimulate plant growth, conserve moisture and suppress the growth of annual weeds. Many materials are suitable — choose the cheapest if it is easy to obtain.

WHAT IT DOES

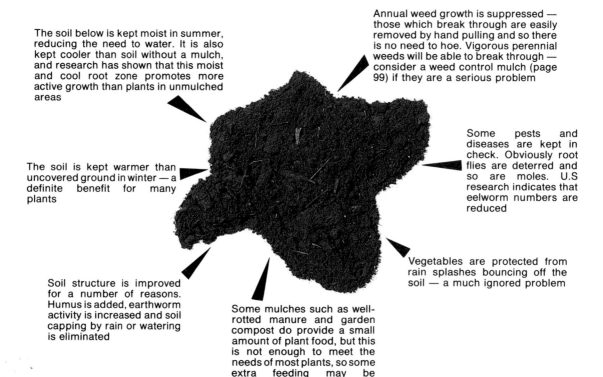

The soil below is kept moist in summer, reducing the need to water. It is also kept cooler than soil without a mulch, and research has shown that this moist and cool root zone promotes more active growth than plants in unmulched areas

Annual weed growth is suppressed — those which break through are easily removed by hand pulling and so there is no need to hoe. Vigorous perennial weeds will be able to break through — consider a weed control mulch (page 99) if they are a serious problem

The soil is kept warmer than uncovered ground in winter — a definite benefit for many plants

Some pests and diseases are kept in check. Obviously root flies are deterred and so are moles. U.S research indicates that eelworm numbers are reduced

Soil structure is improved for a number of reasons. Humus is added, earthworm activity is increased and soil capping by rain or watering is eliminated

Some mulches such as well-rotted manure and garden compost do provide a small amount of plant food, but this is not enough to meet the needs of most plants, so some extra feeding may be needed

Vegetables are protected from rain splashes bouncing off the soil — a much ignored problem

WHAT TO USE

PEAT

Peat is used on both mixed borders and shrubberies — it is widely available and reasonably inexpensive for small areas. Sphagnum peat helps to maintain acid conditions around lime-haters and has a natural look, but when dry it tends to blow about or forms a cake which is difficult to rewet.

BARK or COCOA SHELL

Bark is a better choice than peat. The chips should be ½–2 in. (1–5 cm) long. Cocoa shell is a good alternative but can be smelly when wet. Use them in the same way as peat — they are the most attractive mulches for use around trees and shrubs. Both will last on the surface for 2–3 years.

WELL-ROTTED MANURE

Manure is less attractive than peat or bark as a surface cover, but it is available very cheaply at the farm or stable gate and is the best soil improver of all. It must be well-rotted and quality from an unknown source can be a problem — weed seeds may be present. Annual topping-up is necessary.

GARDEN COMPOST

Garden compost is not only free — it gets rid of grass clippings, soft cuttings, old stems etc. Like manure it provides nutrients and improves the soil structure as well as acting as an insulator, but it is usually less effective. It must be good quality as poor compost is full of weeds. See page 108.

STRAW

Straw is easy and cheap to obtain in rural areas, and is widely used as a mulch both in grand estates and tiny allotments. It is rather unsightly, however, around the plants in a bed or border in the front garden. Two problems — weed seeds are often present and it can only be used with a nitrogen-rich fertilizer.

OLD GROWING COMPOST

Spent peat compost has the virtues and limitations of peat with the added value of having some nutrients present. Examples include the contents of used growing bags, spent tomato compost (suitable for nearly all plants) and spent mushroom compost (not for use around lime-hating plants).

GRASS CLIPPINGS

Short clippings from the lawn can be used as a shallow mulch (no more than 1 in./2.5 cm) — keep away from the crowns of the plants. Top up as necessary during early summer. Two warnings — do not use if flowering weeds were present or if the grass has been treated with a weedkiller.

HOW AND WHEN TO MULCH

Humus mulches are insulators which help to retain the conditions occurring at the time they are put down. This means that the soil should be just right for active growth — warm and moist and not cold and dry.

The standard time for applying a humus mulch is May. Before you begin putting down organic matter it is necessary to prepare the soil surface. Remove debris and hand pull or hoe annual weeds. If these weeds are abundant it is easier to spray with a quick-acting contact weedkiller — see page 91. It is also important to get rid of perennial weeds. Dig out if only a few are present, otherwise spray with glyphosate. The final job is to apply a general fertilizer and rake in lightly.

The soil is moist, warm and free from weeds — it is now time to spread a 2–3 in. (5–7.5 cm) layer of the chosen mulching material over the ground around the stems. This covered area should extend for about 1½ ft (45 cm) around the centre of a shrub and for 2½ ft (75 cm) around the trunk of a moderate-sized tree. If mulching material is plentiful you can cover the whole bed or border, but with both partial and all-over cover you must make sure that the mulch does not come right up to the stems. A build-up of moist organic matter against the shoots can lead to rotting. Do not disturb this layer during the summer months. If weeds do appear pull out by hand or paint with glyphosate gel.

Some people fork in the mulch during October and then allow the soil to warm up in the spring before applying a new mulch. This is a lot of work, however, and so it is more usual to leave the mulch in place and top up as necessary in May.

WHERE TO MULCH
Around Growing Plants

The usual type here is the humus mulch — a multipurpose layer of organic matter to protect the soil surface, cut down the need for watering and weeding and improve the soil structure. The plants which are recommended for mulching are trees, shrubs, roses and hardy perennials. Vegetables are not often given a humus mulch but are sometimes grown through a weed control mulch (page 99) and annuals are either unmulched or surrounded by a thin layer of grass clippings during the summer months. With young trees and shrubs weeds around the stems can be a serious problem, and so a circle or square of weed control mulch is placed around the stem and then covered with gravel or bark chippings. Squares of bituminous felt ('tree spats') can be bought for this purpose.

Over Ground to be Planted

The usual type here is the weed control mulch — done properly it will mean that weeding will be a thing of the past. This type of mulching is perhaps most successful when you are making a new shrub border, although it can be used for a mixed border. It can also be used in the vegetable plot where growth is stimulated, potatoes no longer need earthing up and strawberries, marrows and courgettes are kept off the ground. See page 99 for details.

The Weed Control Mulch

Weed control mulches are forms of organic or inorganic sheeting which suppress perennial as well as annual weeds. The soil surface is protected, the need to water is reduced but improvement to the soil structure is either slight or does not take place.

WHAT TO USE

POLYETHYLENE SHEETING

Black polyethylene ('polythene') sheeting is widely available and is the most popular type of weed control mulch. Standard 150-200 gauge sheeting will only last a single season if not covered (see below) but heavy-duty 500 gauge sheeting will last for several years.

WOVEN POLYPROPYLENE

Woven polypropylene is harder to find than polythene and is about three times the price. Use it in the same way — the advantages are that water seeps through the myriad holes between the threads rather than having to percolate through the edges of the sheet, and it will last for six years or more.

OLD CARPETING

Old carpeting makes an excellent weed control mulch — use as a strip between rows of plants or cut into squares and use as tree spats. It is very easy to lay, but it does need a surface cover if appearance is important. It is long lasting and of course free when you decide to recarpet a room.

CARDBOARD

Cardboard is not often used, but old cardboard boxes are freely available at most supermarkets and can be used as tree spats when cut into squares. Several sheets of newspaper can be used for the suppression of annual weeds. In both cases a cover (e.g bark) is needed.

WHEN AND HOW TO MULCH

An overall mulch can be placed over ground which is to be planted with shrubs, roses, hardy perennials or vegetables. September is a good time to put down the mulch for autumn planting of roses etc, but with the vegetable plot you will have to put down the mulch in spring. The first step is to cut down the weeds with shears or a strimmer — you can spray with glyphosate but complete weed eradication is not essential. Fork in a fertilizer if the soil is not rich and put down slug pellets if this pest is a problem.

Lay strips of plastic across the prepared ground — make sure the edge of each sheet overlaps the one below. Bury the edges in the soil and make slits or cross-cuts in the surface to act as planting holes. Water will move effectively between the sheets and through the slits, but prick the sheeting in areas where puddles form.

Exposed plastic sheeting may be acceptable in the vegetable plot but some form of cover is needed in the ornamental garden. Lay a thin layer of bark chippings, cocoa shell or gravel over the mulch. Gravel makes an excellent mulch on its own — use pea shingle or washed stone chippings.

For individual plant mulching use a square or circle of the sheeting material and cover with bark, peat or gravel.

GROWING GROUND COVER

In the easy-care garden it is essential to blanket bare ground in order to prevent colonisation by weeds. You can put on a non-living blanket (a mulch) or grow a living blanket which is referred to as ground cover. The key property of ground cover is that they are reasonably or highly ornamental plants with a spread of leafy growth which is sufficiently dense to partly or completely inhibit weed development. Most but not all are low-growing and most but not all are evergreen. Most have a fairly controlled growth habit, but some are rampant invaders which people are warned not to use. This warning is only partly correct — if the purpose of the ground cover is to clothe the soil between plants then these rampant ones should be avoided. But another use for ground cover is to clothe inaccessible areas such as banks where little else would grow, and here the vigorous invasive types may be a godsend.

Ground-covering plants can save you the tedious job of weeding for years to come, but it takes both time and care to establish them properly in the garden. First of all you must prepare the planting site thoroughly — all annual and perennial weeds must be killed or removed by manual or chemical means. Next, newly-planted ground cover will be surrounded by bare earth, so mulch them if possible and hand pull any emerging weeds promptly for a couple of seasons. After that the plants should look after themselves apart from a seasonal trimming and occasional hand weeding. A word of warning. Do not try to fill all the bare spaces with ground cover rather than a mulch — if you do the garden will have an overcrowded look.

NAME	TYPE	PAGE NO.
AJUGA	HP : E	48
ALCHEMILLA	HP : D	48
BERGENIA	HP : E	48
COTONEASTER	S : E	32
EPIMEDIUM	HP : SE	48
EUONYMUS	S : E	32
EUPHORBIA	HP : D	48
GERANIUM	HP : D	48
HEBE	S : E	32
HEDERA	S : E	32

NAME	TYPE	PAGE NO.
HEUCHERA	HP : E	49
HOSTA	HP : D	49
HYPERICUM	S : SE	32
JUNIPERUS	C : E	34
NEPETA	HP : D	49
ROSA	S : D	41
SEDUM	HP : E	49
STACHYS	HP : E	49
TIARELLA	HP : E	49
VINCA	S : E	33

NAME	TYPE	NOTES
BALLOTA	HP : E	Grey woolly leaves. Height 1 ft (30 cm), spacing 1½ ft (45 cm)
CALLUNA	S : E	Heather for acid soil. Height 6–18 in. (15–45 cm), spacing 1 ft (30 cm)
IBERIS	S : E	I. sempervirens bears white flowers. Height 1 ft (30 cm), spacing 1 ft (30 cm)
LAMIUM	HP : SE	White-marked leaves for shade. Height 4 in. (10 cm), spacing 1 ft (30 cm)
LYSIMACHIA	HP : D	Creeping Jenny for damp soil. Height 2 in. (5 cm), spacing 1 ft (30 cm)
PACHYSANDRA	S : E	Good under trees. Height 4 in. (10 cm), spacing 1 ft (30 cm)
POLYGONUM	HP : E	P. affine is invasive. Height 1 ft (30 cm), spacing 2 ft (60 cm)
PULMONARIA	HP : D	White-spotted leaves. Height 1 ft (30 cm), spacing 1 ft (30 cm)

TYPE KEY
HP : Hardy Perennial **S** : Shrub **C** : Conifer **E** : Evergreen **SE** : Semi-evergreen **D** : Deciduous

Ajuga reptans 'Variegata'

Ballota pseudodictamnus

Euonymus fortunei 'Variegatus'

Geranium 'Russell Pritchard'

Hosta decorata

Juniperus squamata 'Blue Star'

Lamium galeobdolon 'Variegatum'

Lysimachia nummularia 'Aurea'

Polygonum affine 'Donald Lowndes'

USING THE RIGHT TOOLS

For those gardeners who have the time, energy and inclination to enjoy gardening to the full there may be little to learn from this section. They will already have a collection of well-loved and well-used tools, and will have no great desire to find ways of reducing the physical effort involved in creating and maintaining a garden.

The needs of the easy-care gardener, however, are different. If the area is large then time-saving pieces of equipment are essential, but they must be affordable and also truly useful — some so-called 'aids' actually make more work than the simple tools they replace.

Choose carefully. For the elderly and the handicapped picking the right tools is even more important — it can mean the difference between being able to do a task or not. With spades, forks, hoes, secateurs, shears and so on you must see that both the weight and balance suit you before buying. A spade which is right for a strong youth would be quite wrong for a small frail lady.

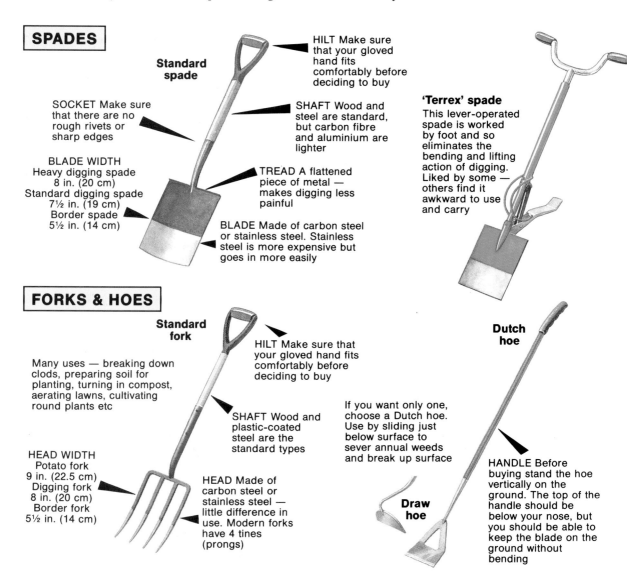

SPADES

Standard spade

HILT Make sure that your gloved hand fits comfortably before deciding to buy

SOCKET Make sure that there are no rough rivets or sharp edges

SHAFT Wood and steel are standard, but carbon fibre and aluminium are lighter

BLADE WIDTH
Heavy digging spade 8 in. (20 cm)
Standard digging spade 7½ in. (19 cm)
Border spade 5½ in. (14 cm)

TREAD A flattened piece of metal — makes digging less painful

BLADE Made of carbon steel or stainless steel. Stainless steel is more expensive but goes in more easily

'Terrex' spade
This lever-operated spade is worked by foot and so eliminates the bending and lifting action of digging. Liked by some — others find it awkward to use and carry

FORKS & HOES

Standard fork

HILT Make sure that your gloved hand fits comfortably before deciding to buy

Many uses — breaking down clods, preparing soil for planting, turning in compost, aerating lawns, cultivating round plants etc

SHAFT Wood and plastic-coated steel are the standard types

Dutch hoe

If you want only one, choose a Dutch hoe. Use by sliding just below surface to sever annual weeds and break up surface

HEAD WIDTH
Potato fork 9 in. (22.5 cm)
Digging fork 8 in. (20 cm)
Border fork 5½ in. (14 cm)

HEAD Made of carbon steel or stainless steel — little difference in use. Modern forks have 4 tines (prongs)

Draw hoe

HANDLE Before buying stand the hoe vertically on the ground. The top of the handle should be below your nose, but you should be able to keep the blade on the ground without bending

RAKES & CULTIVATORS

Rake

HILT Some types have a modelled plastic grip

HANDLE Made of wood, aluminium or plastic-covered metal. Make sure length is right for you before you buy

SHAFT

HEAD Nearly always made of carbon steel or stainless steel

Many types of hand cultivator are available — their purpose is to cultivate the soil to a depth of 2–3 in. (5–7.5 cm). Most gardeners don't need one — forking over followed by raking should be quite sufficient.

Rake

A number of short teeth set in a horizontal plate. Choose a 12 in. (30 cm) wide head with 10–14 teeth

Tined cultivator

Can be bought with removable centre tines for cultivating along rows. Wheeled models are available

Star-wheeled cultivator

Combines several starred wheels with a hoe — it is pushed to and fro to produce a fine tilth

Mattock

Heavy chopping hoe is used to break up the surface of heavy soils. The top may bear a 2-pronged cultivator

POWER CULTIVATORS

A motorised cultivator seems like a good idea — a petrol-driven jack-of-all-trades to take the hard work out of gardening. Unfortunately it will not be of much help in the established ornamental garden. The main value of a motor-driven cultivator to the average gardener is the ability to dig over a large area when creating a new garden. If you are going to make a large vegetable garden as well as other features, then it is worth considering purchasing one of the many models available. If, however, the area is not large and most of the cultivated ground is lawn and ornamental areas, it is a much better idea to hire one if you plan to create a new bed or border in uncultivated ground. This will mean less work than digging, but it will also be less thorough. If you buy one there should be an adequate range of attachments — hoes, picks, ridgers, soil aerators etc.

HAND TOOLS

A **trowel** is essential for planting specimens too small for a spade. It is also used for digging out perennial weeds. Buy stainless steel if you can afford it and make sure the handle is comfortable. Buy two — a standard size one and a small narrow type with a blade about 2 in. (5 cm) across. Look for a strong neck and don't buy a long-handled one unless you find bending difficult.

Hand forks are about the same width as trowels, but bear 3–5 short tines instead of a scoop-like blade. They are used for weeding and cultivating soil around plants — buy a long-handled version to reach to the back of the border. The tines are available in various forms — flat, curved and twisted. Choose a fork with flat tines — the other shapes have drawbacks. The hand fork, unlike the trowel, is not essential.

WHEELBARROWS

The traditional **wheelbarrow** is illustrated above — a 2–4 cu.ft (0.06–0.12 cu.m) container carried on a tubular metal frame and bearing a single narrow wheel. Galvanised metal is the usual material. Plastic wheelbarrows are available — attractive but liable to break if subject to very heavy treatment. Always test a barrow before buying.

The traditional type is highly manoeuvrable and a good choice for heavy, uneven ground. However, to make pushing easier buy one with a wide pneumatic tyre or buy a **ball wheelbarrow** with an inflated, ball-like wheel. If you are not strong or if you are disabled, consider a **two-wheel cart** instead of a wheelbarrow. You will find it easier to push and less liable to tip over.

WATERING EQUIPMENT

The need to water can be reduced by good soil preparation and mulching — see pages 96–99. There are times, however, when the application of water is necessary. A wide range of watering equipment is available — the best choice depends on the size of your garden and the depth of your pocket. The best (and most expensive) system for beds and borders is an underground drip or leaky-pipe arrangement with an electronic on-off tap linked to a soil moisture sensor. Easy-care, but at a price. The tap connecting an underground system to the mains must be fitted with a non-return valve.

Watering can

Impractical for overall watering in anything larger than a tiny garden. Vital, however, for point watering a few plants. Choose the right size and sort of can — 10 litre (2 gallon) with metal rose for garden use and 5 litre (1 gallon) with long spout for the greenhouse

HOSE PIPES

Flat tubing

Lay-flat tubing is lighter than round tubing. It is wound into a cassette-like case for easy storage. A flat hose pipe is worth considering if you are short of space, but it is expensive and must be unwound before use

Round tubing

The basic type which will last for many years if treated properly. A long length should be stored on a wheeled or wall-attached reel. Leaving the hose crushed on the floor can lead to kinks and punctures. Empty and store indoors in winter

Single wall

Double wall

Reinforced

The usual type of hose pipe is made of PVC and is available in 50 ft and 100 ft (15 m and 30 m) lengths. Single wall tubing is inexpensive, but it is not suitable for regions with high water pressure. Double wall tubing is more suitable for general garden use, but reinforced tubing is the best (and most expensive) type you can buy — there is a layer of fibre or braided nylon between the inner and outer tubes. Ribbed tubing is easier to hold than smooth tubing when wet. In recent years Quick Release fittings have largely replaced screw fittings for securing attachments

OVERALL WATERING EQUIPMENT

Sprinkler hose

Basically a flattened hose pipe bearing a series of fine holes on the upper surface. A long rectangular spray pattern is obtained — excellent for grass paths and rows of vegetables

Seep hose

Basically a plastic hose pipe bearing a series of pinholes along the sides. These holes are situated close to plants — the water seeps through these holes to water the ground around the roots. Useful in the shrub or mixed border, but planting areas are limited to the locations of the holes in the pipe

Sprinkler

The simplest type of sprinkler system. The pattern is quite even but the area covered is relatively small, so a series of these fixed watering points is necessary to water a bed or border. For lawns underground sprinklers are available which pop up when switched on — popular in the U.S but not in Britain

Leaky pipe

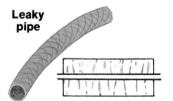

This watering system is an advance on the seep hose. The hose pipe is porous so that water seeps out along its whole length — plants do not have to be set at any particular point along the pipe. Buy in kit form — connect to the water supply with a standard hose and bury the porous hose several centimetres below the soil surface

Drip system

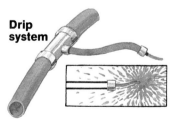

The most sophisticated system of all, especially when linked with an electronic tap to control the water supply. Drip valves are sited close to plants in the border and connected by small-bore flexible tubes to the main supply hose which is buried below ground level. Efficient — water goes only where it is needed

CUTTING TOOLS

There always seems to be a cutting job to do in the garden — dead-heading, trimming hedges, pruning, lopping off branches etc. This can be hard work, but you can make it much easier if you have the right tools. There are four rules. Firstly you must choose the right type of cutting tool for the thickness of wood to be severed and you must then choose the most suitable example of this type — for instance you will find that some secateurs are quite wrong for your hands and needs. Lastly, having decided which tools you want to buy make sure you pick the best quality you can afford and keep them sharp and clean after use.

Garden knife

It is a joy to watch a skilled gardener using a knife for pruning, budding etc, but in the hands of the inexperienced it can be a dangerous weapon. If you have not been trained in its use carry a folding pocket knife for cutting twine and so on, but use secateurs for cutting stems

BLADES Keep cleaned and oiled after use

SAFETY CATCH Make sure that you can reach it easily

SPRING May be exposed or hidden. The handles should open quickly after cutting

HANDLES Check weight and comfort before purchase. Make sure that they are not too big — handles should not push hard against your palm when open

Secateurs vary in size from delicate flower gatherers to large heavy-duty types. You should need only one pair of secateurs — a general-purpose model about 8 in. (20 cm) long. Use them for stems up to ½ in. (1 cm) in diameter.

Anvil secateurs

One sharpened blade cuts on to a flat platform (anvil). Always cut *down* on to the anvil. Cuts with less effort than the curved type, but the cut may be a little more ragged

Curved secateurs

One sharpened blade cuts against a broad blade — side anvil secateurs is an alternative name. Generally last longer than anvil type. The most popular type

Ratchet secateurs

These are the secateurs to buy if you have a weak or painful grip. Only a light squeeze is needed — the stem is partly cut and the ratchet moves the blade forward. Another light squeeze deepens the cut — up to 4 squeezes may be necessary

Long-handled pruner

Ordinary secateurs should not be used on branches which are more than ½ in. (1 cm) across as the tool may be damaged. For cutting ½–1½ in. (1–4 cm) wide stems use a pair of long-handled pruners. The 1½–2 ft (45–60 cm) handles give extra leverage — telescopic-handled pruners are available

Garden shears

The main use is the trimming of hedges, although shears are also used for cutting long grass, dead-heading annuals, trimming perennials etc. Choose a pair with comfortable handles and light-weight blades — holding heavy shears becomes a chore when cutting a long hedge

Hedge trimmer

A wise investment if you have a long hedge to cut. A mains model is suitable if the hedge is near a power point — otherwise buy a battery-operated one. For heavy duty a petrol-driven model may be necessary, but it is heavy to carry. A 1½ ft (45 cm) blade is recommended

Pruning saw

When branches are thicker than a broom handle it is necessary to use a saw rather than an instrument with blades. For the occasional branch you can use an ordinary saw, but many prefer the curved Grecian saw which cuts only on the pull stroke

MISCELLANEOUS EASY-CARE AIDS

Grabber

Picking up piles of leaves or cuttings from the ground usually involves bending over to gather them up between two boards. The grabber is operated from one or both long handles and the need to bend is removed. The grabber edges may be smooth or toothed. Check that the weight and height are suitable before buying

Shredder

Thick woody prunings can pose a disposal problem. Building a bonfire may not be practical and taking them to a dump is time-wasting. An electric shredder turns 1 in. (2.5 cm) wide stems into wood meal which is a good ingredient for making compost — see page 109. Read and follow all the safety instructions

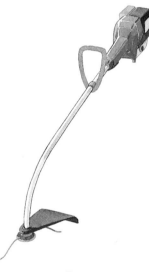

Strimmer

Cutting long grass in areas inaccessible to the mower can be a back-breaking job with a pair of shears. The strimmer makes it quite a simple job — the motor drives a nylon cord rather than a blade. Buy an electric lightweight model unless the area is very large — the petrol version is heavy and very noisy

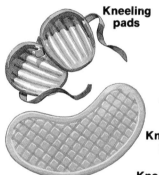

Kneeling pads

Kneeler stool

Kneeling mat

Kneelers

Kneeling on hard ground can be painful for all and damaging for the elderly. Strap-on plastic foam kneeling pads can be used for knee protection, or you can use a kneeling mat. A kneeler stool is useful if getting up and down is a problem. One way up it is a kneeler with arm supports — turn it over and it is a seat

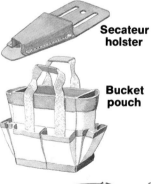

Secateur holster

Bucket pouch

Gardener's pouch

Tool tidy — outdoors

Having to keep on bending down to pick up secateurs, twine, a trowel etc can be tiring — it is much more efficient to wear a gardener's belt or pouch to carry small tools as you move round the garden. The minimum tidy you should have is a secateur holster to keep both hands free at pruning time when you are not cutting branches. Some people prefer to use a bucket pouch rather than a body one, especially during the hot days of summer. This pouch or bag is made from canvas and fits around a 10 litre (2 gallon) bucket — pockets hold gloves, seeds, secateurs, string, hand fork etc

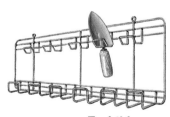

Tool tidy — indoors

All too often tools are left leaning against the wall or on the floor of the garage or shed when not in use. Time is wasted in having to hunt for a particular tool when there is a job to do and there is also the danger of treading on rakes, hoes etc. It is much better to attach a series of galvanised or plastic-coated wire tool racks to the wall

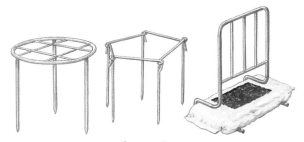

Supports

Supports for weak-stemmed plants should always be inserted before they flop and look unsightly. You can stick to the traditional cane or stake plus string method, but these days there is a range of wire supports which do not need string — they are 1–4 ft (30–120 cm) tall and are useful for Lilies, Paeonies, Delphiniums etc. Several proprietary types of growing bag support are available — buy a stout one for cucumbers and tomatoes

Tip bag

It is not always easy to take your wheelbarrow to all parts of the garden when collecting prunings, leaves, grass clippings etc. A tip bag made from plastic fabric, such as the Bosbag, can be carried about very easily and when full carried to the compost heap, bonfire etc. The bag can be folded and stored flat when not in use

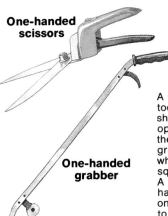

One-handed scissors

One-handed grabber

One-handed tools

A number of one-handed tools are available — shears which are operated by squeezing the handles together and grabbers for pruning etc which are operated by squeezing the trigger. A boon for people who have limited or no use of one hand, but more tiring to use than the two-handed versions of these tools

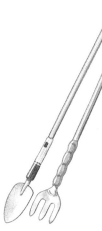

Long-handled tools

A good deal of gardening work involves using short-handled tools and working on your hands and knees. For many people this is not possible because of age or infirmity, and for them there are several ranges of long-handled trowels, forks, weeders etc. The usual plan is to buy a handle with a set of interchangeable heads

Bulb planter

The trowel is the most popular planting tool and is the best one to use if the bulbs have widely different diameters. A bulb planter is often recommended, but it is the preferred alternative only if a number of conditions apply. The soil is moist and not sandy, the bulbs are to be set at approximately the same depth and the long-handled model is chosen to save bending. The planter is pushed in by foot and the plug is removed from the corer by a hand-operated lever

pH meter

When choosing a new plant one of the key considerations is whether the specimen is right for the pH (acidity) of your soil. If the pH is below 7 then the lime-haters will be at home — if above 7 then the lime-lovers will flourish. Until recently it was necessary to use test tubes or test paper to get a rough idea of the pH — now there are gauges fitted with a soil probe which will give you an exact reading for the soil in various areas of your garden

MAKING COMPOST

The need for a plentiful supply of organic matter in order to improve the soil has been stressed in several parts of this book. Relying on shop-bought material is far too expensive a proposition, and picking up free animal manure at the farm or stable gate is only feasible in out-of-town areas and usually in limited quantity.

The answer is to make compost from unwanted plant material. Unfortunately the instructions in many books are based on the use of woody matter such as straw, dead leaves etc. We read about helpful lime, harmful soil, the need to turn and the value of using a nitrogen-rich activator. But in most gardens the starting point is almost entirely grass clippings from the weekly mowing of the lawn, and for grass clippings you have to use a completely different procedure.

What goes in

Successful composting takes place only when there is intense bacterial and fungal activity. Heat is generated and humus is formed. For this to take place you need a mix of material with 30 parts of carbon to 1 part of nitrogen. As a very rough guide, waste plant material which is orange, brown or black is rich in carbon, and material which is soft and green is rich in nitrogen. If you use just grass clippings, green weeds and a few prunings then you will have a mix which contains too much nitrogen for active bacterial growth. The secret of good compost is to incorporate some carbon-rich material as outlined in the 5 step technique on page 109.

In addition to lawn clippings you can use vegetable and flower stalks, leaves, annual weeds, peat, soft hedge clippings, bracken, straw, smashed-up brassica stalks, tea leaves, peelings, household vegetable waste and egg shells. The lawn weedkiller in clippings will break down in 6–9 months if the technique described on page 109 is carried out. Test before using — see below. Do not use twigs, roots of perennial weeds, badly diseased plants or meat and fish waste from the kitchen. If you have to burn non-compostable woody material do make sure that the material is dry so that there are flames rather than dense smoke.

What comes out

Compost made from grass cuttings with some form of insulation and without a rainproof cover is a slimy green mess which has little value in the garden. Compost made by the method outlined here is quite different. The materials slowly change as a result of heat and intense bacterial activity and the compost is ready when it is crumbly and there is no unpleasant smell. It will be brown rather than green and the individual ingredients will not be easily recognisable. Compost started in the spring or summer should be ready in late autumn or the following spring. Autumn compost is for forking into the soil — spring material is excellent for mulching. It is wise to test compost made from clippings from a weedkiller-treated lawn. Mix a sample with some peat and sow cress or radish seed — normal germination indicates that the garden compost is safe to use.

The Container

THE GOOD CONTAINER ✓

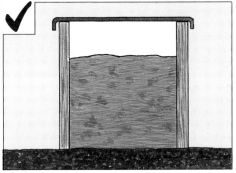

THICK WALLS
Wood, breeze blocks, solid plastic and bricks are all suitable. Keeping the heat in is one of the secrets of making good compost

LARGE
One big one always beats 2 small ones

WATERPROOF COVER
Rain must be kept out of the heap. Use a rigid cover or a sheet of plastic

THE POOR CONTAINER ✗

THIN PLASTIC OR WIRE NETTING
Vital heat is lost — it is this heat which kills weed seeds and breaks down organic matter. Put boards or bags round the sides if you can or lean it against a wall — line wire bins or plastic bags with old newspapers

SMALL
Contents cool down too quickly

OPEN TOP
Rainwater stops bacterial activity — secondary fermentation turns the compost into green, smelly sludge

The 5 Step Way to make Compost

Look carefully at the features of a good container before you begin. It should be as large as practical — you cannot turn a few barrowloads of grass cuttings into true compost.

STEP ONE · PUT DOWN A LAYER OF GREENSTUFF

This layer should be about 9 in. (22.5 cm) deep but an exact depth is not critical. The layer should be flat and not heaped up.

STEP TWO · SPRINKLE ON A LAYER OF CARBON-RICH MATERIAL

This stage is necessary if you are making the heap with soft green material such as grass clippings. There are various carbon-rich materials you can use — wood meal made from prunings ground by a shredder is excellent and so are sawdust, shredded paper and dry leaves. This layer should be about ½ in. (1 cm) thick. Turn into the surface of the greenstuff layer with a fork.

STEP THREE · COVER WITH A THIN LAYER OF SOIL

Forget the traditional advice to keep soil out of the compost heap. This thin soil layer provides a multitude of bacteria, mops up undesirable gases and absorbs water.

STEP FOUR · REPEAT STEPS 1–3

Continue to build up layers until all the clippings etc have been used up.

STEP FIVE · COVER THE TOP

The last step before leaving the heap is to replace the lid to keep off the rain. This step is vital. Repeat steps 1–5 next week when you have another load of grass clippings.

HIRING PEOPLE & EQUIPMENT

The most effective work saver is, of course, to hire someone else to do the work. If you do decide to tackle a large job yourself because of the expense involved in hiring a professional then time and energy can be saved by hiring the right piece of equipment for the task in hand. It sounds easy but hiring people or equipment can be a headache. There are many horror stories about the appalling work and outrageous prices charged by the so-called 'cowboys' and there have been injuries arising from faulty hired equipment. The golden rule is never to save time at the choosing and contracting stages — think carefully and act warily before you hire.

Hiring People

Getting someone to help in the garden may sound like the answer to your prayers, but without forethought it can go wrong. Set out below are the things to look out for.

HIRING A GARDENER FOR GENERAL HELP

- Find out the hourly rate for your area by asking other people, and see if friends can recommend someone they have used
- If you have to find your own gardener then look through local papers or place your own advertisement in the press. Do not give work to people who knock at the door
- Agree the rate in writing and list the work that you will expect to be done
- There can be a tax problem. If you employ your helper for only a few hours a week there should be no problem, but a part-time gardener working just for you may be classed as an employee which will involve you in paying both PAYE and National Insurance. If in doubt, check with the Tax Office
- If you are disabled the local Council may provide garden help free of charge. Check with the Council Office

HIRING A CONTRACTOR FOR A SPECIFIC TASK

- If possible go to a company which has been highly recommended by someone with high standards
- If you have to find your own contractor look through Yellow Pages — get a quote from several if you can
- Agree the job in writing and be as specific as you can. Make sure the landscape contractor is insured and don't keep adding little bits to the job as the final price may go up alarmingly. Get an additional quote if you decide you want extra work done

Hiring Equipment

There may be times when there is a job to do which calls for heavier and more expensive equipment than you have in the tool shed. If the task is a regular one such as cutting a large lawn then you should consider buying a larger mower, or if there are many trees to prune then you should certainly buy long-handled pruners to complement the secateurs. Some big jobs, however, are one-offs — moving a large amount of rubbish, cutting an extensive area of overgrown grass, cutting down a number of trees, turning over an uncultivated plot etc. Hiring the necessary equipment is the answer.

- When hiring, be clear about what you want. Cement mixers, mowers, cultivators, skips, chainsaws, hedge trimmers, conveyors etc come in a range of sizes
- Look at the equipment carefully. Check for loose nuts, missing parts, frayed cables and so on
- Obtain instructions — get a manual if possible or carefully write down what has to be done. Ask for a demonstration if practical
- Make sure that you have the necessary safety equipment
- Look at the contract before signing. Make sure the item is in good condition if that is how it is described

CHAPTER 15

AVOIDING STRAIN & INJURY

Strain and injury are related but are not the same thing. Strain involves wrongly applied or excessive physical movement — injury usually involves an accident rather than pulling, lifting or bending.

The aim of easy-care gardening is to enable you to have an attractive garden with a minimum of effort. Saving time is one of the key features, but there is no point in saving time in the garden only to have to spend considerable time in visiting a doctor or going to hospital as a result of your gardening activity. Don't assume that it cannot happen to you — about 250,000 people every year need hospital treatment as a result of garden-related strain or injury. In nearly every case the cause is either ignorance or carelessness, so do read this chapter to avoid aches and pains or even worse.

Avoiding Injury

There are a few general rules. First of all, get rid of hazards. Level paths which are uneven, fix loose stones, hang up tools, remove dangerous branches etc. Next, make sure that you are wearing correct clothing. It should keep you warm and protected in winter, and cool and protected in summer. The key word is 'protected' — on this page and the next one you will see the role played by clothing in preventing accidents. Make sure that clothing doesn't actually cause an accident — avoid loose bits like scarves and ties when working with fast-moving machinery.

EAR & EYE PROTECTION

Ear protectors are necessary if you are using a noisy power tool for a prolonged period. Remember that the neighbours do not have ear protectors — try to agree with them the best time before doing a really noisy job. Eye injuries are especially distressing so do take simple precautions. Put old yoghurt pots on top of canes, remove stones from the grass before mowing and be careful of twigs and branches when pruning trees. Remember to wear goggles when doing any job which has a history of eye accidents — drilling holes in masonry, cutting tiles or paving slabs, using an axe, using a chainsaw, lopping trees etc.

HEAD & FOOT PROTECTION

Head protection is not usually necessary, but you will need an industrial hard hat if you are planning to lop off large branches which are more than head-high. Feet are different — you must protect them when doing a range of standard jobs such as forking, digging and mowing the lawn. Sandals and trainers are out — choose instead stout shoes, boots or wellingtons. Winter foot-wear should be warm and completely water-proof. Do keep your mind on the job when using a fork or a lawn mower. Pushing a garden fork through one's foot is an all-too-common occurrence — each year 4,000 accidents involving a fork require hospital treatment.

HAND PROTECTION

Gloves are necessary to protect your hands when undertaking many gardening tasks, and you may need more than one type — leather ones for dealing with roses and cotton ones for non-prickly jobs. Most people compromise by using a pair of all-purpose gloves — fabric ones with leather or thick plastic palms. You should wear gloves when handling soil as broken glass, broken pots etc can result in a nasty gash, but there are times when work is much easier when your hands are bare. If you are a regular gardener and you just cannot seem to avoid picking up cuts and scratches, a routine anti-tetanus injection is a good idea.

Don't leave cuts to look after themselves — wash out any dirt immediately with soap and warm water after which the wound should be covered with a porous elastic dressing. Do not use an airtight plaster. Remove splinters and thorns with a needle which has been sterilised by immersion in boiling water. Most cuts need neither a doctor nor hospital treatment, but if blood loss is excessive then seek medical help immediately. This also applies if a home-treated cut starts to hurt after a day or two or the surrounding area becomes swollen or discoloured.

ELECTRICAL DANGERS

Electricity outdoors has its own special rules and you won't learn these from your experience with fitting plugs to table lamps. Carefully read the following points. Check the lead and plug before use — there should be no frayed wires or loose connections. Leads and connectors should be outdoor quality and make sure the cable is over your shoulder before you switch on a hedge trimmer or lawn mower. Always switch off and unplug if you have to do any cleaning, adjusting or stopping for a tea break. Above all have a circuit breaker to cut off the current if the equipment becomes live. The type to buy is a Residual Current Device (RCD).

CHILD PROTECTION

As an easy-care gardener you will probably regard the garden as a place in which to relax rather than somewhere in which to work all the time. A place where the children can run freely, but the sombre fact is that 100,000 children each year are treated in hospital as a result of garden mishaps. Between the ages of 2 and 5 children are active with little sense of danger. Tools and machinery should be kept out of reach — so should chemicals, flammable liquids and other home-care products. Tell them that paths are for walking and lawns are for running. Keep paths clear and do teach young children not to eat any berries, leaves etc.

You must make sure that small children can't wander into the road. In most gardens this calls for secure fencing and a gate which can be locked beyond the reach or ability of small fingers. Glass and children don't mix — both can harm each other. Balls can break glass — glass can cause horrific injuries. Keep the greenhouse far away from the play area — consider safety glass, plastic or wooden sides. Do not allow a child under 3 to go near an unguarded pond or in a paddling pool without supervision.

MISCELLANEOUS DANGERS

The main site of accidents in gardens is on **paths** and driveways — you must therefore pay attention to these areas. Keep all paved areas in good repair — level uneven stones and secure loose slabs. Keep clear of toys, rubbish, wet leaves, slimy mould and algae. Use a path & patio cleaner if necessary. A few garden **plants** can cause stomach upsets and other undesirable effects when the berries, seeds or other parts are swallowed. Warnings now appear on the labels, but your best safeguard is to avoid eating anything which is not a recognised fruit or vegetable. Plant allergies are much more common than cases of plant poisoning — do wear gloves when handling plants which have an allergy warning on the label. Parasites occur in about a quarter of cat and dog **droppings**. They rarely affect humans but you should dispose of animal droppings promptly without touching them. Using **ladders** calls for safety measures — do keep children away. Place the feet on a firm and straight surface so that the distance from the wall is about a quarter of the height from the ground to the top. Store and handle **chemicals** carefully.

Avoiding Strain

Falls are the major cause of gardening accidents requiring hospital treatment, but it is back strain which is by far the most common reason for discomfort and days off work. Do read the instructions below even if you are an experienced gardener — few people know all the rules.

BEFORE YOU BEGIN	Spring is the worst time for strains, as any physiotherapist will tell you — muscles have often been inactive for months and the weather is cold. It is therefore a good idea to carry out a simple exercise programme. Bend over and stretch back several times while standing with legs apart. Bend side to side and tense your buttocks for 10 seconds. You are ready to go.
WHEN YOU ARE WORKING	Make sure your clothing is right — you should be warm without any part of the back being exposed to cold winds. Try to remain as upright as possible with the back arched. Kneeling instead of stooping is the golden rule, and never jerk suddenly to pull up a weed or lift up a load. Try to vary the heavy jobs — don't do a strenuous task for more than half an hour at one time.
AFTER YOU HAVE FINISHED	Clean the tools, put them away and don't flop in a chair — muscles must be stretched to avoid backache next morning. Sit upright in a straight chair with a rolled-up towel between the back of the chair and the small of your back. After a strenuous session in the garden it is better to lie on your back and raise your left leg and then your right one several times.

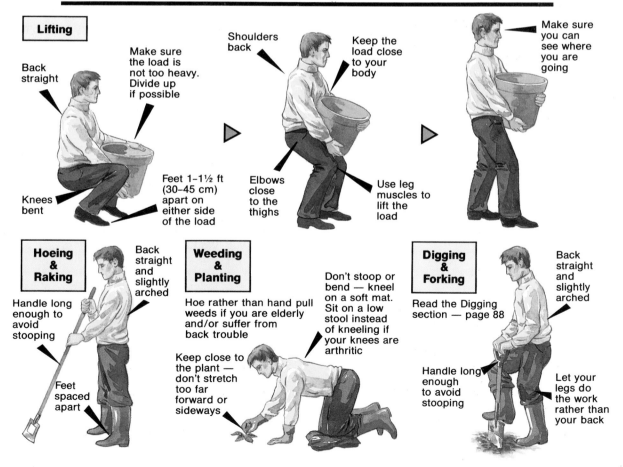

Lifting

Back straight

Make sure the load is not too heavy. Divide up if possible

Knees bent

Feet 1–1½ ft (30–45 cm) apart on either side of the load

Shoulders back

Keep the load close to your body

Elbows close to the thighs

Use leg muscles to lift the load

Make sure you can see where you are going

Hoeing & Raking

Handle long enough to avoid stooping

Back straight and slightly arched

Feet spaced apart

Weeding & Planting

Hoe rather than hand pull weeds if you are elderly and/or suffer from back trouble

Don't stoop or bend — kneel on a soft mat. Sit on a low stool instead of kneeling if your knees are arthritic

Keep close to the plant — don't stretch too far forward or sideways

Digging & Forking

Read the Digging section — page 88

Handle long enough to avoid stooping

Back straight and slightly arched

Let your legs do the work rather than your back

CHAPTER 16

INCREASING YOUR STOCK

In a standard gardening textbook this chapter would be largely devoted to the raising of new plants from seeds or cuttings in either seed or multipurpose compost. This work is done indoors in containers covered with glass or transparent plastic to ensure a moist atmosphere. The seedlings and rooted cuttings are transplanted into small pots and then hardened off for their life outdoors.

Raising new plants under glass can be a lot of fun, but it is also a lot of work. The standard way in which the easy-care gardener increases his or her stock is by obtaining plants at the right season from the garden centre, DIY store, nursery, market stall or occasionally by mail order. The yearly round begins in spring when shrubs, hardy perennials and roses are bought in containers or as bare-root specimens to fill gaps in the garden or to replace plants which died in the previous season. A little later when the frosts have passed the bedding plants are bought in packs or strips for planting in beds, borders and containers. During summer further shrubs, roses and perennials are bought on the basis of their floral beauty at the garden centre and autumn/early winter is the end of the buying year. This is the time for planting bulbs, roses, shrubs and perennials to provide colour in the following spring or summer.

This reliance on brought-in material as the way to increase the stock in the garden is of course more expensive than raising your own plants, but it is generally agreed to be much less time-consuming and less risky. This is not necessarily so — there are several very easy techniques whereby you can raise new plants out in the garden without any need for pots, seed compost, propagators, greenhouses, cold frames or any of the other paraphenalia of the dedicated propagator.

Do try at least one of these easy propagation techniques as there are several advantages. There is the satisfaction of having plants which are actually home-grown and have not been raised by somebody else. In addition these new plants have started their lives in your ground and so do not have to make the sometimes difficult move from peat-based compost to your less friendly soil. You can grow seeds of annuals which are not available as bedding plants from your garden centre and lastly, but certainly not least, there is the purely practical advantage of saving money.

SOWING SEEDS IN THE GARDEN

Most vegetables are grown from seed sown directly in the soil and then thinned as necessary. Growing flowering annuals from seed sown in the garden is often frowned upon as an easy-care technique. The seed bed has to be weed-free, watering is necessary in dry weather and thinning is often required. There are situations, however, where outdoor seed sowing is child's play. A number of easy-to-grow hardy annuals such as Candytuft, Limnanthes, Viscaria, Echium and Californian Poppy can be grown by scattering seed very thinly over moist soil in March or April. When the seeds are large (e.g Sweet Pea and Nasturtium) simply push the seeds into the soil in spring and then fill the holes.

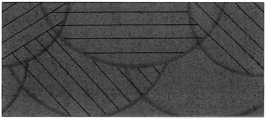

Choicer annuals need to be thinned after sowing. When growing several types mark out zones for each variety with a sharp stick — see above. Draw shallow drills and sow very thinly. Rake the soil back, firm it and after emergence thin the seedlings to the required distance.

DIVIDING CLUMPS

Some hardy perennials and bulbs can be raised from seed but the usual method here is to divide up large clumps. With perennials choose a mild day in spring or autumn when the soil is moist. Dig up the clump with a fork and break it up into well-rooted pieces. You may be able to do this with your hands, but if the clump is too tough for this technique then use two hand forks or garden forks. Push the forks back-to-back into the centre of the clump and prise gently apart. Select the divisions which came from the outer region of the clump — discard the central dead region. Replant the divisions as soon as possible and water in thoroughly.

LAYERING

Some small shrubs such as Lavender, Vinca and Ceratostigma form clumps which can be split up like hardy perennials and the pieces replanted, but shrub propagation nearly always leaves the parent plant undisturbed. Shrubs with flexible stems can be raised very easily by layering — some plants (e.g Rhododendron and Magnolia) produce new plants naturally by this method. To layer a shrub or climber, a stem is pegged down in spring or autumn and left attached to the parent plant until roots have formed at the base of the layered shoot. This takes 6-12 months. Suitable subjects include Berberis, Camellia, Clematis, Forsythia, Heather, Japonica, Lilac, Lonicera, Magnolia and Rhododendron.

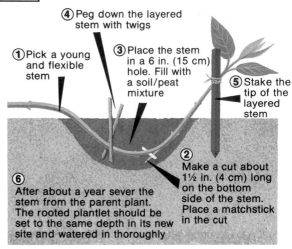

④ Peg down the layered stem with twigs
① Pick a young and flexible stem
③ Place the stem in a 6 in. (15 cm) hole. Fill with a soil/peat mixture
⑤ Stake the tip of the layered stem
② Make a cut about 1½ in. (4 cm) long on the bottom side of the stem. Place a matchstick in the cut
⑥ After about a year sever the stem from the parent plant. The rooted plantlet should be set to the same depth in its new site and watered in thoroughly

PLANTING SUCKERS

Shrubs are often expensive, so it is worth considering one of the ways of propagating daughter plants from a choice specimen in your garden. Some woody plants spread by means of suckers, which are shoots which arise from an underground shoot or root. Leaves arise where the sucker roots in the soil, and removing and then planting this daughter plant is the easiest method of propagating shrubs. Examples of suckering shrubs include Corylus, Cotinus, Mahonia, Pernettya and Symphoricarpos. The best time is early winter for deciduous plants and April or September for evergreens.

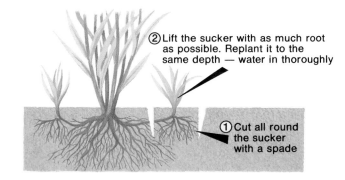

② Lift the sucker with as much root as possible. Replant it to the same depth — water in thoroughly

① Cut all round the sucker with a spade

TAKING HARDWOOD CUTTINGS

A cutting is a small piece removed from a plant which with proper treatment can be induced to form roots and then grow into a specimen which is identical to the parent plant. Many hardy perennials and most shrubs are propagated in this way — softwood cuttings (green at the top and base) are used for perennials and some small shrubs and semi-ripe cuttings (green at the top and partly woody at the base) for shrubs, climbers and conifers. These cuttings are taken in spring or summer and are placed in compost in an enclosed container.

For the easy-care gardener who does not want to be bothered with compost, cold frames etc hardwood cuttings are the answer. The time to take and plant these cuttings is late autumn, using well-ripened shoots of this year's growth. Vigorous roses and bush fruit can be propagated in this way, and so can the following shrubs: Aucuba, Buddleia, Buxus, Cornus, Deutzia, Forsythia, Jasminum, Ligustrum, Lonicera, Kerria, Laburnum, Philadelphus, Populus, Potentilla, Ribes, Salix, Sambucus, Spiraea, Symphoricarpos and Weigela.

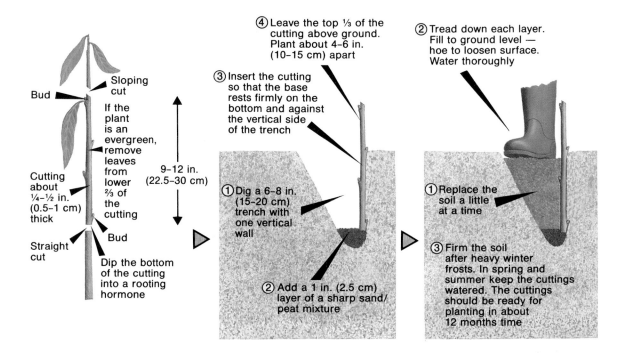

Bud

Sloping cut

If the plant is an evergreen, remove leaves from lower ⅔ of the cutting

Cutting about ¼–½ in. (0.5–1 cm) thick

9–12 in. (22.5–30 cm)

Straight cut

Bud

Dip the bottom of the cutting into a rooting hormone

④ Leave the top ⅓ of the cutting above ground. Plant about 4–6 in. (10–15 cm) apart

③ Insert the cutting so that the base rests firmly on the bottom and against the vertical side of the trench

① Dig a 6–8 in. (15–20 cm) trench with one vertical wall

② Add a 1 in. (2.5 cm) layer of a sharp sand/peat mixture

② Tread down each layer. Fill to ground level — hoe to loosen surface. Water thoroughly

① Replace the soil a little at a time

③ Firm the soil after heavy winter frosts. In spring and summer keep the cuttings watered. The cuttings should be ready for planting in about 12 months time

CHAPTER 17

TROUBLES

There is no reason why the easy-care gardener should suffer more from plant troubles than the dedicated active gardener who spends a great deal more time in the garden. It is also nonsense to believe that pests and diseases only attack badly-grown plants. However good the beds and borders may appear there will always be some unwelcome invaders — the insect pests and fungal diseases which attack plants and can spoil all your efforts.

The nature of the plant is important here, and one of the features of the easy-care types recommended in earlier chapters is that they tend to be less susceptible to problems than many trouble-prone varieties recommended in standard textbooks. Roses which are unduly susceptible to mildew and black-spot are omitted, and so are vegetables which are particularly prone to problems.

Weeds are a major headache alongside pests and diseases, and once again the easy-care gardener scores. Mulching is one of the key techniques set out in this book, and one of its main purposes is to keep down weeds in beds and borders.

On the following pages you will find a frightening array of pests and diseases and on page 90 there are just a few of the weeds which may appear in your garden. It is not the purpose of this rogue's gallery to frighten you as you are unlikely to see more than a few of them. It is much more likely that your plants will be harmed by an enemy from within rather than by an outside marauder. These disorders are many and varied — see page 125.

The golden rule for having healthy plants is to prevent trouble before it starts — many of the easy-care techniques are designed to do that. In addition you should deal with any problem as soon as you see it, but as stressed on the next page this does not mean spraying everything in sight.

PESTS
Animals, varying in size from microscopic eel-worms to majestic deer, which attack plants. The general term 'insect' covers small pests — mites, slugs, woodlice and true insects such as aphids. See pages 119–122

DISEASES
Plant troubles caused by living organisms which are transmitted from one plant to another. Fungal diseases are the most common but there are other diseases caused by bacteria and viruses. See pages 123–124

DISORDERS
Plant troubles which may have disease-like symptoms but are not due to a living organism — they are caused, not caught. Common causes are too much shade, too little food, frost, waterlogging and drought. See page 125

WEEDS
Plants growing where you do not want them to be — no plant is inherently a 'weed'. Self-sown annual flowers in a rose bed are weeds — dandelions in a wild garden are not. All broad-leaved plants are weeds in a lawn. See pages 26 and 90–92

Keeping Plants Healthy

PREVENT TROUBLE BEFORE IT STARTS

- **Prepare the ground thoroughly** Pull out the roots of perennial weeds when cultivating soil prior to planting. If the soil is in poor condition you must incorporate organic matter. This will help to open up heavy soil, where water-logging in winter is a major cause of root-rotting diseases. It will also help sandy soil by building up the water- and food-holding capacity.

- **Choose the right plants** There are three separate points to think about here. Firstly, choose an easy-care variety if you can. Next, make sure the plant is suited to the site. Avoid sun-lovers if shade is a problem, do not pick tender types if the garden is exposed and prone to frosts, and forget about acid-loving plants if the ground is chalky. Finally, buy good quality stock as described in Chapter 2. Reject soft bulbs, lanky bedding plants and disease-ridden perennials.

- **Plant properly** You have chosen the right plants and the soil is in a fit state to receive them, but trouble lies ahead if you don't follow the rules for good planting in Chapter 2. These rules ensure that there will be no air pockets and that the roots will spread into the garden soil in the minimum possible time.

- **Remove rubbish, weeds etc** Rotting plants can be a source of infection — some actually attract pests to the garden. Boxes, old flower pots and so on are a breeding ground for slugs. Weeds rob plants of food, water, light and space.

- **Follow hygiene rules under glass** The humid atmosphere of a greenhouse is a paradise for pests and diseases. Control is often difficult, so prevention is better than cure. Use compost or sterilised soil. Ensure the house is adequately ventilated — dry air encourages pests and saturated air encourages diseases. Try to avoid sudden fluctuations in temperature. Water regularly. Remove dead leaves and plants immediately.

- **Feed properly** Shortage of nutrients can lead to many problems — poor growth, undersized blooms, lowered disease resistance and discoloured leaves. Take care — overfeeding can cause scorch. The new slow-release fertilizers are very useful for the easy-care gardener.

TACKLE TROUBLE WITHOUT DELAY

- **Examine dead plants** Don't just throw them away after lifting — look at the soil ball and the ground which held the plant. If roots have not developed from the original soil ball, then re-read the planting instructions in Chapter 2. If there is an infestation of grubs in the soil, consider using a soil insecticide before replanting.

- **Cut out dead wood** When pruning in autumn or spring cut out all dead and badly diseased wood and burn it. If a large canker is present on a branch of a tree cut back to clean wood.

- **Don't try to kill everything** Not all insects are pests — many are positive allies in the war against plant troubles. Obviously these should not be harmed and neither should the major part of the insect population — the ones which are neither friends nor foes. There will be times when plant pests and diseases will attack, but even here small infestations of minor pests can be ignored (e.g cuckoo spit) or picked off by hand (e.g caterpillars, rolled leaves and leaf-miner damaged foliage).

- **Spray if you have to** Spraying is called for when an important pest is in danger of getting out of hand. Pesticides are safe to use in the way described on the label, but you must follow the instructions and precautions carefully. A bewildering array is offered by most garden shops — look at the label carefully before making your choice. The front will tell you whether it is an insecticide (page 119), a fungicide (page 123) or a herbicide (page 91). Make sure that the product is recommended for the plants you wish to spray. If it is to be used on fruit or vegetables check that the harvest interval is acceptable. Do not make the mixture stronger than recommended. The easy-care approach to spraying is to buy a ready-to-use solution packed in a trigger-operated container.

The leaves should be dry and the weather should be neither sunny nor windy. Use a fine forceful jet and spray thoroughly until the leaves are just covered with liquid which is just beginning to run off. Do not spray open delicate blooms.

After spraying wash out the equipment, and wash hands and face. Do not keep any spray solution you have made up until next time and store packs in a safe place.

Below-ground & Surface Pests

PEST	BACKGROUND	CONTROL
CABBAGE ROOT FLY	Young cabbages, sprouts, radishes, turnips etc die — older ones are stunted. Leaves are blue-tinged. Look for small white maggots on the roots	Place a collar around the base of each seedling when planting out if you are really bothered. Lift and destroy affected plants
CARROT FLY	A serious pest of carrots and parsnips. Seedlings are killed — mature roots are riddled and liable to rot. Look for reddish leaves and for small creamy maggots in the roots	Try to avoid thinning — the smell of crushed leaves attracts the flies. Next year sow in March or June
CUTWORM	Large grey or brown caterpillars just below the surface. Young plants are attacked at night — stems are severed at ground level	July-August is the danger period. Hoe around affected plants — destroy caterpillars brought to the surface
LEATHERJACKET	Dark grey grubs — 1 in. (2.5 cm) long and slow moving. Can be a problem on the lawn — look for brown patches and intense bird activity. May also be serious in new, badly-drained plots	Tackle the problem when digging and hoeing. Pick up and destroy the easily-recognisable grubs
ONION FLY	Small white maggots burrow into the bulb bases — young plants are killed, old ones fail to develop. Look for yellow, drooping leaves	Try to avoid thinning — grow sets or transplants. Destroy damaged leaves. Firm the soil around the plants
SLUGS & SNAILS	Serious garden pests, especially when the weather is wet and cool. They hide under debris during the day and come out at night, devouring seedlings and roots, stems, leaves and even flowers. Slime trails are a tell-tale clue	Remove rubbish and hand-pick at night, but you will need a slug killer if attacks are bad. Metaldehyde pellets are popular, but you must use them properly. *Never* put down heaps — spread thinly around the plants. Store the pack safely
VINE WEEVIL	An important pest of container plants — look for white grubs in the compost	Pick out and destroy if seen — use a nematode-type insecticide
WIREWORM	A pest in newly-broken grassland — ½ in. (1 cm) long shiny, yellow grubs attack the roots of many plants	Avoid growing potatoes and root vegetables for about 3 years in infested land. Destroy grubs when digging

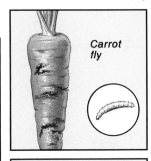

Carrot fly

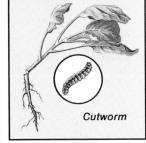

Cutworm

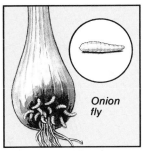

Onion fly

Slugs & snails

INSECTICIDES

These chemicals are used to control insects and other small pests. There are 3 basic types of active ingredient — the product you buy may contain 1, 2 or even all 3 types.

INSECT-CONTACT INSECTICIDES

For most sap-sucking insects such as green-fly and capsid. They work by hitting and killing the pests — spray during and not before the attack. Use a forceful jet and cover all parts of the plant. Example — malathion.

LEAF-CONTACT INSECTICIDES

For plant-chewing insects such as caterpillars. They work by coating the insects' source of food. You do not have to hit the insects, but you must obtain good cover of the leaves. Spray at the first sign of attack. Example — fenitrothion.

SYSTEMIC INSECTICIDES

For sap-sucking insects and some caterpillars. They work by going **inside** the plant and into the sap stream. New growth after treatment is protected and hidden insects are killed. Good cover is not essential. Example — permethrin. Some products contain systemic and contact insecticides.

Above-ground Pests

PEST	BACKGROUND	CONTROL
APPLE SAWFLY	A ribbon-like scar appears on the skin. A creamy grub is inside — sticky 'frass' surrounds the surface hole. Fruit usually drops in July	Pick up and destroy fallen fruit. Use a spray a few days after petal fall if you are really keen
BLACKFLY	A serious pest of broad beans in spring and French beans in July. Large colonies stunt growth, damage flowers and distort pods	Pinch out tops of broad beans once 5 flower trusses have formed. Use pest pistol if serious
CATERPILLARS	Many types attack plants — usual sign is the presence of large irregular holes in the leaves. Cabbage white butterfly can be serious	If practical pick off by hand. Where damage is widespread use insect spray or pest pistol
CODLING MOTH	Pale pink grubs inside fruits of apples, pears and plums in July and August. Sawdust-like 'frass' surrounds eaten-out area	Live with it. The only practical alternative is to use a chemical spray programme
CUCKOO SPIT	Frothy white masses on the stems of many plants. Within are pinkish froghoppers which suck the sap	Wash off with a forceful jet of water if you wish, but not worth bothering about
EARWIG	A pest which can attack vegetables and fruit — chrysanthemums and dahlias are the major targets. Leaves and petals are torn	Shake plants — destroy earwigs which fall. Trap in upturned flower pots filled with straw
EELWORM	Microscopic worms which affect leaves, stems and/or roots of numerous plants including chrysanthemums and potatoes	No cure — do not replant for 3–6 years if you are sure eelworms are present
FLEA BEETLE	Tiny yellow and black beetles which jump when disturbed. Small round holes appear in young leaves of the cabbage family	Live with it, or use insect spray if the attack is serious
GREENFLY	An all-too-familiar pest — green, brown, yellow or pink. Rapid build-up in warm, settled weather. Young growth is weakened — viruses are transmitted	Water plants in dry weather. Spray greenfly clusters with pest pistol or insect spray
LEAFHOPPER	Small green insect produces pale mottled patches on leaves of ornamentals, e.g pelargonium. Direct damage is slight but viruses are transmitted	Spraying is not worthwhile
LEAF MINER	Winding tunnels, blisters or blotches occur on the leaves of many plants, including chrysanthemums and carnations	Pick off and destroy mined leaves
MEALY BUG	An indoor pest, infesting house plants and greenhouse ornamentals. Clusters of cottony fluff occur on stems and the underside of leaves	Deal with the trouble promptly. Wipe off with a damp cloth or a moistened cotton bud
PEA & BEAN WEEVIL	Young peas and beans can be killed or severely retarded by the small beetles which bite notches in the leaves	Hoe around plants in April and May. Use insect spray if the attack is severe

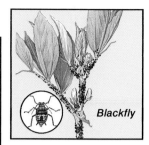

Blackfly

Codling moth

Chrysanthemum eelworm

Flea beetle

Leaf miner

Pea & bean weevil

PEST	BACKGROUND	CONTROL
PEA MOTH	The cause of maggoty peas. Eggs are laid on the leaves in summer — the greenish grubs bore through the pods and into the seeds	Early- and late-sown crops usually escape damage. Otherwise use insect spray 7–10 days after flowering starts
RASPBERRY BEETLE	The cause of maggoty raspberries, loganberries and blackberries. The grubs can soon ruin the crop	If attacks occurred last year, use insect spray when the first fruits start to turn pink
RED SPIDER MITE	A general pest of greenhouse and house plants. Leaves turn an unhealthy bronze — fine silky webbing is a tell-tale sign	Encouraged by hot and dry conditions. Damp down under glass. Use insect spray if necessary
ROOT APHID	Greyish 'greenfly' and white powdery patches occur on the roots. Many plants can be affected but lettuce is the favourite host	There is no cure. Lift and destroy affected plants. Grow aphid-resistant lettuce variety (e.g Avoncrisp)
ROSE SLUGWORM	Areas of the leaf are skeletonised. Affected areas turn brown. Greenish grubs on surface	Pick off affected leaves. If serious use insect spray
SCALE	Non-moving insects which attack a wide range of plants. The small discs are found on stems and the underside of leaves	Wipe off with a damp cloth or a moistened cotton bud
THRIPS	Silvery flecking and streaking occur on flowers, leaves and pods. Minute black or yellow flies are just visible	Not usually treated
WASPS	A nuisance in the garden as ripening tree and soft fruits are damaged. Only blemished fruit is attacked	Live with the problem. If close to the house it may be necessary to destroy the nest
WHITEFLY	A serious greenhouse pest — clouds of small moth-like flies in the air and greenish larvae under the leaves	Chemical control is difficult — hang up yellow greenhouse fly catchers
WINTER MOTH	Green 'looper' caterpillars devour the young leaves of fruit trees. Petals, flower stalks and fruitlets may also be attacked. Leaves are often spun together	Encircle each trunk with grease bands if you are really keen
WOOLLY APHID	A pest of ornamental and fruit trees and shrubs — the white waxy wool on the stems is produced by the aphids within	Rub or scrape off — brush large areas with an old toothbrush and methylated spirits

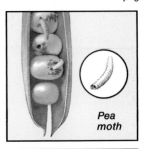

Pea moth

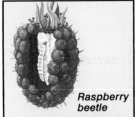

Raspberry beetle

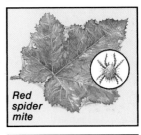

Red spider mite

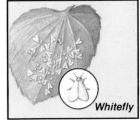

Whitefly

Woolly aphid

Animal Pests

A number of animals can damage your garden, but the approach to them must be different to the way we tackle insect pests. The object here must be to protect the plants and/or discourage the invaders without causing them actual harm. There are exceptions — rats must be killed and the mole too, if all else fails.

PEST	BACKGROUND	CONTROL
BIRDS	The flower garden is least affected — only Polyanthus, Primula wanda and Crocus are stripped of buds and flowers. Vegetables can suffer badly, especially peas and the cabbage family. Seeds and seedlings are eaten, sparrows tear flowers and pigeons strip away the soft portion of leaves. Bullfinches and sparrows devour buds of cherries, gooseberries etc — the fruit is also attacked	Small areas can be protected with soft plastic netting — make sure all the plants are covered and the base of the net is properly secured. For a large number of plants a fruit cage is undoubtedly the best answer. Spray-on repellents are of limited value and are removed by rain — mechanical scarers soon lose their ability to frighten away birds
CATS	Cats are a pest of the flower and vegetable garden. Seed beds and young transplants are disturbed by their scratching	Protection is not easy if cats have chosen your flower bed as a toilet. Try one of the newer cat repellent sprays or a sonic deterrent
DEER	Deer can be a serious pest in rural areas close to woodland. Young trees are grazed — the bark may be stripped in winter. Rose buds are a favourite meal	Tall fencing is the real answer but may not be practical. Ring the trunks of trees with fine-mesh wire netting
DOGS	Dogs, like cats, will scratch in soft ground. Remove dog droppings at once — they are a health risk. The most serious effect, however, is the brown patches caused on lawns by bitch urine	Hedges and prickly shrubs will deter stray dogs. Try one of the newer repellents. Copiously water affected areas on the lawn
FOXES	A new but not serious pest in urban areas — plants are not attacked but dustbins are disturbed	Do not leave plastic bags containing waste food standing out overnight
MICE, RATS & VOLES	Mice, rats and voles attack stored fruits and vegetables — in the garden whole rows of larger seeds such as peas may be removed	Rats *must* be destroyed. If you see one then get in touch with the Council. Use racumin for mice and voles
MOLES	An invasion by moles can cause havoc. Severe root damage occurs and the hills thrown up by their tunnelling are unsightly. Small plants may be uprooted — the lawn is most at risk — the surface is disfigured and uneven	Begin with simple remedies. Moles dislike soil disturbance — try a mechanical scarer. Next, try an anti-mole smoke. If all else fails you may have to call in a professional exterminator
RABBITS	Rabbits are very fond of young greens, but in winter they will gnaw the bark at the base of trees. A serious problem in rural areas — they can easily burrow underneath ordinary fencing	Individual tree guards can be used, but an anti-rabbit fence is the only complete answer. The wire netting should be 3 ft (90 cm) above ground, and 6 in. (15 cm) below
SQUIRRELS	Nice to watch, but they can be a nuisance. Bulbs, soft fruit, nuts etc are removed and bark is stripped in winter	There is little you can do. Fruit netting helps and wire-netting guards will protect individual trees

Birds

Cats

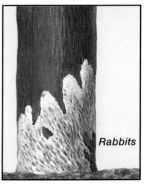

Moles

Rabbits

Diseases

DISEASE	BACKGROUND	CONTROL
APPLE SCAB	Appears first as dark green or brown spots on leaves. Fruits are cracked and disfigured with corky patches	Rake up and remove fallen leaves. Prune scabby twigs
BACTERIAL CANKER	A serious disease of cherries, plums and other stone fruit. Gum oozes from the bark — affected branches soon die	Cut out diseased branches. Spray with copper in autumn
BLACK SPOT	A major rose problem — black spots with yellow fringes on the leaves. Premature leaf fall often takes place	Rake and dispose of all fallen leaves in winter — apply a mulch in spring. Put on Systhane as leaves open and again in summer if you are keen on roses
BROWN ROT	Apples are susceptible. Fruit turns brown and concentric rings of yellowish mould appear on the surface	Destroy all affected fruit promptly. Store only sound fruit and inspect at regular intervals
BULB, CORM & TUBER ROTS	Browning and decay of underground storage organs	Dry thoroughly before storing. Discard any soft or rotten bulbs
CANKER	A serious disease of apples and pears which can be fatal. Bark shrinks and cracks in concentric rings	Cut off damaged twigs. Cut out canker from stems and branches
CLUB ROOT	Swollen and distorted roots are the tell-tale sign of this disease of stocks, wallflowers and all the cabbage family. Leaves wilt in sunny weather	Make sure land is adequately limed and well-drained. Destroy diseased plants — do not grow cabbage family plants for several years
DAMPING OFF	The most serious seedling complaint. The base of an affected plant becomes withered and blackened — the stem topples over	Use sterilised compost, sow thinly and never over-water. Remove affected seedlings
DIE-BACK	A common problem with woody plants such as roses, fruit trees, ornamental shrubs etc. Die-back spreads slowly downwards from the tip	Cut out all dead wood. Try to improve drainage
DOWNY MILDEWS	Less likely to be troublesome than powdery mildew in the ornamental garden, but it can be serious on the vegetable plot. Upper leaf surface turns yellow — greyish mould occurs below	Make sure the soil is well-drained — practice crop rotation of vegetables. Pick off diseased leaves
GREY MOULD (Botrytis)	Grey and fluffy mould appears on stems, leaves, flowers and soft fruit. Worst outdoors in a wet season and in unventilated damp conditions under glass	Avoid the basic causes — poor drainage, over-watering and inadequate ventilation. Remove affected leaves and fruit

Apple scab

Tuber rot

Club root

Damping off

Grey mould

FUNGICIDES

These chemicals are used to control fungal diseases. Nearly all are preventatives rather than cures. This means that the first spray must go on at the first sign of disease and then be repeated as instructed. With black spot on roses the most important spray is put on months before the symptoms are due to appear. A few fungicides (e.g carbendazim) are systemic and enter the sap stream, but they will not clear up a bad infection. Fungicides are mainly for the dedicated rather than the easy-care gardener.

DISEASE	BACKGROUND	CONTROL
LEAF SPOT	Blotches, spots or rings appear on leaves — especially celery and black-currant. Leaves may fall early	Feed with a fertilizer containing potash. Pick off diseased leaves and avoid overcrowding
PEACH LEAF CURL	Large reddish blisters develop on the foliage of peaches, cherries, apricots etc. Unsightly, and the tree is weakened	There is not much you can do, so expect attacks every year. Pick off and destroy affected leaves promptly
POTATO BLIGHT	Spreading brown patches appear on the leaves and infected tubers rot in store. Attacks occur in warm, wet weather	You can spray but it is not usually worth it. Remove infected stems a fortnight before lifting. Inspect the stored crop
POTATO SCAB	Ragged scurf patches occur on the tuber surface. The disease is only skin-deep — eating quality unaffected. Worst on light land	Use compost but not lime before planting. Grow a resistant variety
POWDERY MILDEW	A general menace all round the garden. White powdery deposit occurs on the leaves, stems, buds and fruit. Worst in hot, dry weather. Serious on roses	Mulch in spring and water during dry periods in summer. Spray with carbendazim if you are proud of your roses
ROOT & FOOT ROTS	Many plants, especially vegetables, can succumb. Leaves wilt and turn yellow — roots and sometimes the stem bases blacken and rot	Avoid cold and overwet conditions. Use a sterile compost. Rotate vegetable crops. Lift and destroy infected plants
RUST	Raised pustules (orange, brown or black) appear on the leaves. Numerous plants may be attacked, but rose rust is the one to fear — attacks may be fatal	Use a fertilizer containing potash. Remove affected leaves. If roses are attacked you must use the modern systemic Systhane
SOOTY MOULD	A black fungus which spots or covers the upper surface of the foliage. Grows on the honeydew deposited by sap-sucking pests	Wash off if unsightly. Control by spraying or dusting to get rid of greenfly etc
STEM ROT	A brown patch develops at or near the stem base — roots are not affected. This disease can be serious on tomatoes	Disinfect the greenhouse between tomato crops. Cut out diseased area if attack is slight. Remove and destroy plant if badly affected
STORAGE ROTS	Soft grey or brown sunken areas appear on apples and pears in store	Discard unsound fruit at storage time. Remove and destroy diseased fruit promptly
TULIP FIRE	Scorched areas occur on the leaves — flowers are spotted. Young shoots are covered with a grey mould and the bulbs rot	Diseased shoots should be cut off just below ground level. There is no cure
VIRUS	All sorts of distortions, discolorations and growth problems are produced, depending on the plant	No cure. Destroy infected plants if you are sure of identification. Keep sap-sucking insects under control
WHITE ROT	The leaves of onions and leeks turn yellow and wilt. Fluffy white mould appears on the base of the bulbs. Worst in hot, dry weather	Rotate crops. Destroy diseased plants — do not replant with onions or leeks for at least 8 years
WILT	Leaves wilt even in moist soil and tissue inside stems is often stained brown	No cure — do not grow susceptible plants in the same soil

Peach leaf curl

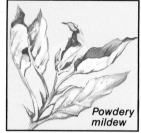

Powdery mildew

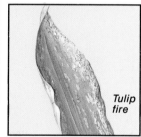

Rust

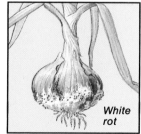

Tulip fire

White rot

Wilt

Disorders

Not all troubles are caused by pests and diseases — split tomatoes and bolted beetroots do not appear in the pest charts but they are still the effects of important disorders. These disorders are due to faults in cultivation or an adverse environment. It is important to try to find the cause because many can be prevented once you know what went wrong. Important disorders and their causes are listed below, but there are others. Blindness of tulips and daffodils is usually due to planting undersized bulbs, and the forking of carrots is due to poorly prepared ground or the use of fresh manure.

DISORDER	BACKGROUND
BOLTING	A number of vegetables have the annoying habit of occasionally bolting or running to seed. The cause is a set-back to steady growth, so try to avoid checks. Prepare the soil properly, plant out firmly and at the right time and make sure the plants are watered in dry weather. Lettuce, onion, celery and beetroot are prone to bolting — grow a bolt-resistant variety if you can
DROUGHT	See page 94
DRY AIR DAMAGE	In the home or greenhouse the effect is a browning of leaf tips. Both outdoors and indoors the most obvious result is a poor set of vegetables which form fruit or pods — tomatoes, beans etc
FROST DAMAGE	With non-hardy plants frost threatens life itself — transplant or sow when the danger of frost has passed. A hard frost can damage the tender new growth of hardy plants such as potatoes, asparagus, apple etc. Affected leaves may be bleached, blistered, cracked or scorched along the margins. The worst effects of frost are seen in the fruit garden — blossom turns brown and drops off
INCORRECT PLANTING	Incorrect planting can lead to slow development or even death of transplants. Inadequate soil consolidation and loose planting lead to several distinct disorders in the vegetable garden — blown brussels sprouts, heartless cabbages, button-headed cauliflowers etc
IRREGULAR WATERING DAMAGE	The outer skin of many vegetables hardens under drought conditions, and when heavy rain or watering takes place the sudden increase in growth stretches and then splits the skin. This results in the splitting of tomatoes, potatoes, carrots etc. Avoid by watering before the soil dries out. A common disorder due to the irregular watering of growing bags is blossom end rot — a sunken, dark-coloured patch appears at the bottom of tomatoes
MAJOR NUTRIENT SHORTAGE	See page 7
SUN & HEAT DAMAGE	Bright sunshine can damage plants grown under glass. Leaves and fruit may be scorched — the pale papery patches are referred to as sun scald. The answer is to apply shading material such as Coolglass in summer
TRACE ELEMENT SHORTAGE	Leaf discoloration is a common symptom. Iron and manganese deficiency lead to yellowing between the veins — the effect is most marked in non-acid soils
WATERLOGGING	The plant is affected in 2 ways. Root development is crippled by the shortage of air in the soil. The root system becomes shallow, and also ineffective as the root hairs die. Leaves turn pale and growth is stunted. The second serious effect is the stimulation of root-rotting diseases
WEEDKILLER DRIFT	Traces of hormone lawn weedkiller can cause severe distortion of tomatoes and members of the cabbage family. Tomato leaves become fern-like and twisted. Fruit is plum-shaped and hollow. Apply lawn weedkiller on a still day. Never use weedkiller equipment for any other purpose
WIND DAMAGE	Wind is often ignored as a danger to plant growth, yet a cold east wind in spring can kill in the same way as frost. More frequently the effect is the browning of leaf margins. Another damaging effect is wind rock, which can lead to rotting of the roots

Frost damage

Irregular watering damage

Manganese shortage

Sun & heat damage

CHAPTER 18

PLANT INDEX

Acknowledgements

The author wishes to acknowledge the painstaking work of Gill Jackson, Paul Norris, Linda Fensom and Angelina Gibbs. Grateful acknowledgement is also made for the help or photographs received from Heather Angel, Pat Brindley, Colin Bailey, Harry Smith Horticultural Photographic Collection, John Glover/The Garden Picture Library (front cover), Michael Howes/The Garden Picture Library, Martine Mouchy/The Garden Picture Library, Clay Perry/The Garden Picture Library, J S Sira/ The Garden Picture Library, Gardening Which?, Bluebridge Farm Studio, Joan Hessayon, Honda Power Products and Nortene Ltd.

John Dye provided both artistry and design work.